Praise [
CLIPP
A mom invents a way to h
just as the world
by Adrienne Alitowski

"*Clipped* is the incredibly detailed adventure of one woman's battle with the ups and downs of product invention. Adrienne is David to the Great Recession's Goliath, representing all of the small business owners who were trying to make their dreams come true during the most severe economic and financial meltdown of our times. But her infectious positive attitude means you never stop rooting for her. Even when it feels like all may be lost, she always finds the riches that truly matter the most."

Carrie Preston: Emmy Award-Winning Actor
(*True Blood, The Good Wife, Claws*)/Director /Producer

"Be forewarned: when you read Adrienne Alitowski's new memoir *CLIPPED: A mom invents a way to hold her life together just as the world falls apart,* you may find yourself literally laughing out loud—or gasping in sudden self-recognition. The author describes herself with endearing self-deprecation as having become "a crazed mom with a mission" and readers will surely relate to her feelings—the triumphs, the disasters, and through it all the ferocious love of an exhausted but indefatigable mom. CLIPPED is a compellingly relatable memoir."

Rachel Vail: (Best-Selling Author
of *Sometimes I'm Bombaloo*)

"Generations have grown up believing in the American Dream—that optimism and hard work will eventually pay off. That's how author Adrienne Alitowski approached the invention and marketing of her product blankyclip—a cute, useful toy to keep stroller blankets in place. What began as a bright idea turned nightmarish in the face of corporate realities and a global recession. With winning humor and refreshing candor, Alitowski spins a universal cautionary tale about what is and what isn't in our control. And ultimately, what really matters."

Sheri Holman: (Best-Selling Author of *The Dress Lodger*
and Screenwriter for *Longmire*)

More Praise For

CLIPPED

"Honest. Tenacious. Ambitious. These words come to mind when describing Adrienne Alitowski, the author of *Clipped*. I was instantly drawn to Alitowski's story. As a mother, I related to her desire to create the perfect baby product that would spare future mothers hours of aggravation (and many loads of laundry). As a professional, I admired her problem-solving skills and determination to launch her business. As a woman, my heart ached as I turned each page and learned how she tackled monumental problems and handled them with grace and dignity. This page turner will draw you in right from the beginning as you root for Alitowski's success."

Carol Bellino: Writer/Producer, CBS Marketing

"*Clipped* is a fascinating chronicle of how a global recession affected one mother's dream of starting a business. Alitowski weaves international headlines into her own story to masterfully build tension around her narrative of motherhood and entrepreneurship. Her candidness and charming sense of humor make this a must-read for anyone interested in how a moment of inspiration can lead us on the most unexpected of journeys."

April Dávila: (Author of *142 Ostriches*)

"An intriguing story of personal invention in the face of the global financial crisis. Thoughtfully written, immersive and insightful."

Sarah Tinsley: (Writer/Founding Member of Women Writers Network)

"A funny and honest read for every aspiring 'Mom-ventor' out there with a great product idea, Alitowski's tale of mixing mothering and entrepreneurship will have all business-minded moms both enthusiastically agreeing and empathizing with her story."

Melissa Fenton: (Writer for *AARP* and *Grown & Flown*)

"A highly entertaining story illuminating the pitfalls and victories of being an inventor and mother during a very dark economic time. You will be rooting for her to the very last page and beyond."

Jan Steele: (Best-Selling Author of *Shoes on the Stairs*)

"Alitowski's book engaged me from the very beginning. A page turner, emotionally engaging, and brilliantly written, I highly recommend this book as a must read. We may face insurmountable challenges, but this book actually delivers!"

Lois Letchford: (Best-selling author of *Reversed: A Memoir*)

clipped

A mom invents a way to hold her life together
just as the world falls apart

a memoir

by
Adrienne Alitowski

FROM THE TINY ACORN ...
GROWS THE MIGHTY OAK

This is a work of nonfiction. The names of some people have been changed to protect their anonymity.

For Gary, Eli, and Dagny

I carry your hearts

"Life is either a daring adventure, or nothing."

—Helen Keller

Prologue

Having a baby at my age—or any age—ends your life as you know it. But Gary and I had been married for seven years, together for eleven, and we wanted children.

It was 2003, and I was thirty-seven. Since my body wasn't going to be endlessly fertile, it was now or never. I couldn't imagine it being never. So I became a mother, and my life did change in every way possible. Thirty-seven years of making myself the priority. Of planning my days around what I needed. Of sleeping. And suddenly I was spending many hours of *all* my days pushing my baby around neighborhood streets in his stroller.

Eli was a baby who needed to be moving, or he wouldn't sleep. Getting those crucial naps in meant staying in motion and keeping him in a safe little cocoon that I made by hanging a blanket over the stroller.

Which brought me to the next oh-so-fun dilemma: How did I keep him in this safe little cocoon when his blanket kept falling off the stroller? Or if I managed to pile enough stuff on top of the stroller to secure one end of the blanket, then the other end would fly in and hit his face. And *wake* him. An extra annoyance came when the blanket fell and hit the street and ended up under the wheels, getting streaked with dirt.

Clearly, what I needed was a clip that would "hold a blanket fast to any model stroller, car seat or carrier but won't pinch little fingers! True security at last," as *L.A. Parent* magazine would say some years later. But I'm getting ahead of myself.

Before nausea and prenatal vitamins entered my life, I worked as an actress mostly. If you were paying attention, you might have seen me on *Beverly Hills, 90210; Just Shoot Me!; Everybody Loves Raymond;* and *18 Wheels of Justice.* Although the odds of succeeding in the entertainment industry are infinitesimal, there was nothing I wouldn't try. I performed a one-woman show; I produced a show, *Glen Mary Glen Rose: Women Do Men,* with celebrity actresses as a fundraiser for breast cancer research; and I directed a short film that played in festivals from Sarasota to Santa Cruz. I thought that if I just held on to that pant leg of life with all my might, my tenacity and fearlessness would land me a juicy role on a must-see sitcom, and my problems would be over. I devoured trade magazines like *Variety* and *The Hollywood Reporter.* I went to seminars and networking breakfasts to learn tidbits that might help me get that next job. I auditioned for anything and everything. I said I played the cello, which I hadn't done since high school, and that landed me a job "playing" in a Don Henley music video (the music was prerecorded, thank goodness). My point is, I was determined, and I loved pursuing an acting career.

But when I went on my first nauseous, pregnant audition and pretended I wasn't pregnant, I could smell—like a poopy diaper under a brand-new onesie—the writing on the wall. And when I dropped off my newborn at a friend's house and ran to audition for a commercial (which I actually booked), it felt wrong to desert him and his needs and be focused back on mine. Without my permission, my priorities had shifted. I was now in the "I'm a mom and it's not about me anymore" phase of life.

There's a reality to how you spend your days with a newborn. At any moment, all day long, every day, food/poop/sleep must be tended to. My baby boss didn't pay me or acknowledge me in any way, and while I wanted to be there for him completely, I did feel torn as this new mother version of myself emerged. I didn't want to feel stuck, but sometimes I did. Having a family had always been a priority for me, and I was so grateful to get pregnant at an age when that's not so easy for women to do. But at the same time, along with the gratitude that I could be there to raise my baby, I felt like a lonely, floating island, unable to leave my house at will. I didn't have an employer to give me maternity leave. This was my new job.

The questions that really plagued me: Will my baby grow up and be grateful I'm doing this for him? Will he be proud of who I am? Will he understand that before he was born I was on some great TV shows and that getting those gigs was an incredible achievement? Maybe he wasn't ready to answer these questions for me since he wasn't yet speaking. Or at all concerned with my angst. Still, my biggest question was: How will I define myself if I am no longer the person I was before he was born?

As exciting as it was to get a small part on *Will & Grace* a couple of months after giving birth, I found myself sharing pictures of Eli with the cast and wanting to talk about him to anyone who would listen. My heart was home with him. Still, at the end of a day alone with a baby, it's easy to feel completely fried and nipple-sore in your messy apartment. If I'm being honest, my mind did take me to very dark places. It was my fault if he didn't sleep or couldn't breastfeed well. I was longing for grown-up conversation, longing to be valued. Didn't I once have my own thoughts? Hard to remember when you're sleep deprived.

It's serious business this baby raising.

<hr/>

One day, in the fog of exhaustion and anxiety that can be mother-hood, I was out and about with Mr. Push Me Or I Won't Sleep. His blanket slipped off, and it hit me: If I could buy so much of what I needed (and so much more that I didn't) to make this mommy gig go smoothly, why couldn't I buy a clip that was safe for babies and could keep the darn blanket from falling off the stroller? I searched every corner of Target, Babies "R" Us, baby boutiques, and the internet. Nothing. And yet, for those struggling with breastfeeding, there were all kinds of helpful products to buy— including a bottle in the shape of a mother's boob. (Don't peek in my kitchen cabinets, please.)

The term "mom inventor" was one I had heard thrown about, and it intrigued me. Could this be my new identity? A mom inventor? It had a nice ring to it. It was a job title that had the connection to motherhood I needed. And so I began the journey to invent, create, patent, manufacture, and sell my idea—just a few short years before the world fell apart in 2008. We know a lot now about how the big banks created a worldwide recession, but mine is a story of its impact on ordinary folks pursuing our dreams alongside what was happening in the world of big business completely unbeknownst to me and about seven billion other people.

Which is not to say that there weren't unexpected riches in store for me, far surpassing my wildest dreams.

1

A Million-Dollar Idea

February 10, 2004. It's a Tuesday. And because I live in Southern California, a February Tuesday is a day when I can push Eli around the neighborhood for a nap.

February 10, 2004, is a slow news day. Bush and Kerry are trading barbs on the campaign trail. *The Da Vinci Code* is still at the top of the bestseller list. The international situation is dire, as it always seems to be, but maybe not as dire as in the recent past. The stock markets creep higher, nothing dramatic. I'm vaguely aware that the Dow Jones is over 10,500 points, which is 600 points higher than when Eli was born two months ago. A sign of good things ahead, I guess. The news of the world is very distant to me as I curse the streaks of dirt on Eli's fallen blanket.

February 10, 2004, is also the day I come up with the idea for blankyclip. Not the name, just the product concept. After pushing Eli around in his stroller for two months, trying to keep the blanket draped over it so he can sleep, I've boiled to a point of raging frustration. If necessity is the mother of invention, then raging frustration is the mother of the mom inventor. When Eli's blanket falls off (again) and ends up under one of the stroller wheels (again!) and gets filthy

(AGAIN!), I realize that a baby-safe clip intended to secure a blanket to a stroller is definitely something I need, and I haven't been able to find one. So I decide to create one.

⁂

Eli may have been why I thought of the product, but he's also why I can't rush out and do anything about it until I have this mommy gig figured out a bit. So, eight months later, I meet with a patent attorney who tells me that in order to file a patent I will need a prototype.

"If you want to bring this blanket clip concept to life, it has to be actualized by someone who takes ideas and turns them into real things you can hold. Once you have this prototype, we can begin the process of applying for a patent. We need the prototype because we'll need to have drawings made, to show what the thing is made of, how its parts work, and why it deserves a patent. In great detail," she adds sternly.

I nod from across the patent attorney's polished desk.

"But I'm not sure this clip deserves a patent, since there are plenty of clips in the world already," she informs me.

Excuse me? My clip is unique and serves an important function and it deserves a patent, I say (to myself). And how do I know this? Because I am a new mom, and I have searched and scoured the baby stores and the internet. There is *no* clip that is safe for babies. There is *no* clip that has loose tension, and is padded, and can clip onto a food tray, and is easy to use. No such clip anywhere out there. Well, at least in the U.S. I confess that I did not search the entire planet.

Yes, there are clips you can buy to close your chip bag and lift your bangs out of your eyes and hold your papers together when you're not ready for the full-blown commitment of a staple. But there's not a single clip that will go over the sunshade of my stroller and also clip onto the food tray where I keep Eli's snacks. I want to be able to clip my blanket onto *both* these stroller parts, and there is no clip that

opens wide enough to do that, that can go over tubing, and that is
both mom- and baby-friendly. A black binder clip or an orange pony
clamp are not going anywhere near my stroller or my baby.

So yes, there are other clips. But my idea is unique, and I'm willing
to plow forward with applying for the patent. Ergo, I need a prototype.

The guy I call tells me he's happy to build my idea, but he wants
the kind of money that companies making movies and commercials
think nothing of. Thousands of dollars! I ask if this guy knows of
anybody who might do it for *not* thousands of dollars, and he says he
knows a guy. And what a guy this next guy is.

I'll call him Tim, since that's his name. There are plenty of people
in this story who will show up as heroes or saviors and will turn out to
be—well, not heroes or saviors, and I won't use their real names. But
Tim gets his real name in this story. He's one of those guys who makes
you feel like you need to go back to kindergarten and learn how to be
nicer because he is just so nice. He operates from a workroom that was
once his garage. He builds amazing dollhouses and toys for his
daughters. He's a dad to make any other dad look bad. Tim knows I
don't have much money, so he is really reasonable, asking only a few
hundred dollars—and he is brilliant.

He also lets me be a big pain in the ass as I ask him to make lots of
tweaks. I'm very picky about what we are creating together. This clip
is my first invention. I don't always know how to get where we need
to get, but I do know when it feels wrong. Being an inexperienced yet
detailed person no doubt makes me one of his worst clients, but I
always come to see him with lots of enthusiasm, and I think he's
amused by me. Or at least he fakes it well, because he never drops the
nice-guy face.

I explain that in my idea for the clip, what makes it possible to
attach it to the stroller frame and even the plastic food tray, is its
S-shaped body. The clip will be really easy to maneuver because the

tension of the coil inside the clip requires only a light amount of pressure to operate.

"So what we need to do," I tell Tim, "is figure out how much foam it takes to make the clip baby-safe without keeping it from functioning properly. I want the entire clip covered, and I want extra foam where the two ends of the clip meet and hold the tension. Babies like to explore, and I don't want that to be a problem." I am filled with passion.

Tim does all the work of building my prototype except the final step of sewing the fabric, but he finds an amazing seamstress. The prototype needs to be fully covered in fabric and to look as polished as possible. I'm so glad he's given this piece of the job to someone who can do it right.

By the time Tim calls to tell me that my prototype is ready, Eli is eleven months old. I first had the idea for this invention when he was two months old. Nine months already! I'm moving much slower with what I now refer to as my "mommy brain." Between the hormonal changes and the sleep deprivation, it's a wonder I've come this far. Nine months after having an idea, I feel like I've given birth again as I hold that gorgeous prototype in my hand. It looks so professional. It's exactly what I'd hoped for. It's soft and opens wide and can clip a blanket to a stroller. Like lots of other new moms, I am so proud and in love with my new blanket clip baby.

My patent attorney explains to me that I'll need to have a non-disclosure agreement form that everyone I'm about to talk to about my blanket clip absolutely has to sign. By signing this document, they promise to keep quiet about my invention. "There are no exceptions," she warns. "Otherwise, you won't be protected in the event that someone tries to steal your idea." If I end up in court one day to defend my idea, I'll need to produce all my NDAs and show how responsible I've been about protecting myself against invention stealers.

The patent attorney makes me sweat. She's so vivid as she describes me in a courtroom talking to a judge that I can hear the gavel striking and the bailiff shuffling his sensible shoes. She goes on and on about how I may need to prove that there's no way I let my idea slip out, and that this awful company/person/multinational juggernaut has stolen my idea and needs to be held responsible.

"If the judge thinks you have been negligent and not asked people to sign these NDAs, your case will be thrown out. You will *not* be protected," she tells me in no uncertain terms.

It is all about the NDA.

There are plenty of people I want to talk to about my invention. For one thing, I'm proud of it. And for another, I need to raise start-up money. But first I need to run home and find an NDA form on the internet as fast as humanly possible. As it happens, it's easy to find a free NDA form online. I make lots of copies and put them in my notebook, vowing to keep my lips sealed until I have those suckers signed.

Then begins the hard part.

You wouldn't believe how testy people can get about signing an NDA. Downright belligerent, some of these folks turn out to be. You might as well be telling them, "I have no trust in you. You will never keep my idea a secret. You are so scummy, and that's why I need a legal document to share this with you." But my lawyer makes me promise I'll have *everyone* I talk to sign one.

Including my family.

It is a scientific fact that family is the hardest group of people to get to sign an NDA. Ridiculously hard. When I fax it to my brother, I can practically hear the snickering over the electronic garble as it comes back signed. One relative who won't be named actually hangs up the phone after he screams an obscenity at me. He stops talking to me as well. This is how badly my NDA and I offend him. The fact that a lawyer has made it clear that this is just standard protocol makes no difference to him. I have asked for the unthinkable. It will be years before he and I speak again.

An old friend of mine from college tells me, "I never sign NDAs." *Huh?* She is just against them. Philosophically. Spiritually. She also stops talking to me (forever) after that conversation. I can't believe how powerful this little form is. It can end relationships in a flash. Fortunately, most people understand and sign the document. My notebook is soon bursting with fully executed NDAs as I begin to share my idea.

I continue to spend a lot of effort on research. If something similar exists, my idea won't find a home in the marketplace. If someone has patented something similar, I won't get that all-important intellectual property protection. So I go to stores—big, small, and in-between—and look at every clip on the market. And not just baby stores, but hardware stores and office supply stores and department stores. (Research is a great excuse to go to lots of different kinds of stores. Nope, no clips at Anthropologie!) But I do go mainly to baby stores in search of a product that might do what my invention does. I study any baby item that clips onto a stroller. I go to libraries and search their databases for anything else I can find about patents and clips. I go through books in the research department of the main library to learn whatever I can learn about starting a business or getting a patent or being a crazed mom with a mission. Apparently, there are a lot of us.

I get myself educated about what's already out there, and it's overwhelming. I read the back of every package—baby products and office products and anything in any store, it doesn't matter—to see if it lists a patent or not, to see where the product is made, to see who makes it, and to see if it's trademarked. And I keep lots and lots of notes. I start collecting the wrong kind of clips in order to show how necessary the right one I've invented is. It becomes a fun little project, to see how dangerous and non-child-safe a clip I can find.

CLIPPED

When I see parents pushing a stroller, using a wooden clothespin or a black binder clip or even an electrical pony clamp to secure their blankets to said stroller, it gives me a secret thrill. They think I'm just a mom pushing a baby in a stroller with all her groceries hanging off the handlebars and shoved in the storage area underneath. They have no idea that I'm also up to something big, and that soon I'll be the reason they don't use black binder clips any more.

It's December 2004. Eli's now a year old! Sarah, a woman from my mommy support group, and her husband buy a home nearby. I'm happy for them as we visit. My son scrambles around the new hardwood floors with his one-year-old playmate. But to be honest, there's some jealousy too. Gary and I still rent an apartment and have no plans (or means) to buy a house.

Sarah tells me, "Banks are giving away loans like hotcakes! Home-ownership in the U.S. is at an all-time high, and you really don't need a whole lot of money to get one." I'm hoping the banks will keep on giving and we can get in on this tidal wave of home loans soon. I grew up in a house that my parents owned in a New York City suburb, but right now that seems like a fantasy for my husband and me.

TOO GOOD TO BE TRUE

December 2004. Housing prices escalated, and yet more and more people were able to buy a house. Historically low interest rates helped those new buyers out, as did banks willing to extend mortgages at below the prime lending rate. These "subprime" mortgages became more and more popular. Freddie Mac got in the game too. And new homebuyers were happy. And the banks that profited from subprime mortgages were happy. And the financial institutions that bought the subprime mortgages in the secondary market or were highly leveraged in mortgage-backed securities (*ahem*, Bear Stearns and Lehman Brothers) were happy. And all was good.

Ah, my mommy support group. I met Sarah and the other members in a prenatal yoga class (because it's LA!), and we had our babies around the same time and suddenly found ourselves desperately in need of support.

The life you live prior to having a baby, the hanging out with childless friends who aren't tied down by disembodied peeps from a baby monitor, becomes more and more difficult to hold on to. Unless you're lucky enough to have someone you can count on, someone who is loyal to you and your new child, someone who can match your baby's energy, someone who has the instincts of an experienced mother and the calm of a grandparent. Of course, I'm referring to a nanny.

I do not have one of these, and both of Eli's grandmas are three thousand miles away. I have not achieved the fame and fortune that my one-woman show and my festival-favorite short film were supposed to yield so my kid could be on some set with me. Gary is doing all he can just to hold on to his job with a golf club company in the manu-facturing world.

So my mommy group becomes an important part of my new life. We discuss how our babies sleep (unpredictably), eat (ravenously), and poop (impressively). We commiserate over our newfound exhaustion and lack of fashion sense. And we also listen to each other's plans for what's next. These women are the first to sign my non-disclosure agreement. We all need these kinds of people—people who will effortlessly sign your NDA and tell you how amazing you are.

I'm so happy I can tell friends and family about my invention now that I have these NDAs ready for them to sign. On the line where I have to fill in what I'm asking them to keep confidential, I write "baby stroller clip," which is how I refer to my invention until I decide on "the blanket clip." But I discover from the trademark office that you can't trademark a name as general as that, so I scribble all possible combinations of the words "blanket" and "clip" on scrap paper, and I come up with "blankyclip." I love this name. In the course of my research and my store stakeouts, I have discovered that the names of most items marketed for young children are all in lowercase letters, so I don't capitalize my invention's first letter. I do a search to make sure it isn't already taken, and then, in February 2005, I apply for my trademark.

The auto-response I receive from the United States Patent and Trademark Office tells me that I'll hear from an examining attorney in six months. That seems like forever, and I figure I'll probably have my blankyclip licensing deal set up by then. Even with a prototype and a product name, I continue to do my patent research on the USPTO website. Clips. Padding. Tension. Baby items. There's no end to how much you can read and explore in the zillions of patents that are already published. I'm digging for something I'm hoping I won't find.

I return to my patent attorney. Now I have a notebook full of patents featuring clips in one way or another. I show her how different my clip is going to be. There is no patent for an S-shaped clip that will go over stroller tubing and food trays. There is no loosely tensioned clip that will be safe for a baby to play with. There is no clip that is fully padded and covered so that no part of it can harm the baby.

Then my endlessly encouraging patent attorney tells me, "In order for us to continue these conversations, I'll require a retainer," which is a cold splash of water to remind me that I'm not chatting with a girlfriend. She does admit, as she's ushering me out of her high-rise office, that my "child-safe fastening device" (as the patent will eventually be called to give my intellectual property even more protection) has a completely different function from any patent I found in my research. Amen, sister!

Now I'm faced with the undeniably real situation that getting further with my invention is going to require more money than I'd anticipated. We're talking lawyers' fees, patent application filing fees, more work on the prototype . . . I'm not sure how much I'll need, but I'm guessing it's more than the none I have.

I reach out to the obvious first target, family. For some lucky people, that's where the search ends. Not so for this mom inventor. I even have a dentist in the family, and dentists are supposed to be the biggest suckers when it comes to raising money, but my dentist says no. And so does everyone else who shares my DNA. They will be proud to see me succeed, but their money certainly isn't going to be part of that process. Bummer.

I turn to friends. Friends see you for who you are passionate about becoming, not who you were in first grade. Friends believe in you and love you and have chosen to be in your life. I decide to create a presentation to show them why it's a good idea to invest in blankyclip.

One of the things that a one-year-old is really good at is keeping his mother one hundred percent occupied. To believe that I can sit quietly and figure out how to put together my presentation while Eli is around is to believe in Santa and the Tooth Fairy and other fantasies that will soon reappear in my life. I break down and hire a babysitter for a few hours each week. I find a low-key diner called Silver Spoon in West Hollywood. It's been a neighborhood landmark for decades, and it's a great place to work during these precious babysitter hours. It has big red Naugahyde booths and walls covered with movie posters and photos of the old stars. I go to my favorite booth, a bit tucked away, and settle in with a cup of tea and my notebooks. I see mostly the same customers week after week, median age about seventy.

When I'm not sure what to write next, I find that staring at the circular glass display with its spinning eight-inch-high cakes is a nice diversion. Who can possibly eat one of those enormous slices? How hungry do you have to be at the end of your meal to order one for dessert? Cake is a nice reason to not think about my invention for a few minutes, but when I come back to my cakeless reality and stare at my text, I realize that I need photos for my PowerPoint presentation.

I'm now at Tim's every couple of days for prototype work, and Eli is enjoying these visits. It's a bit surreal that the baby I was pushing around in a stroller, the baby who was instrumental in my creating my invention, is now big enough to explore and play in the backyard of my prototype builder's home. We live in a building without a yard, so this is a real treat. Eli's in no rush to leave and feels very comfortable with his new friend Tim. He is, after all, the incredibly social baby who's been nicknamed by our friends and neighbors "The Mayor."

In addition to the peace and solitude of those paid-for moments at the Silver Spoon, I'm grateful for any nap that Eli takes. By now he's napping in a crib, so I'm able to use some of this time to work on my presentation. While I sometimes hope I can get some work done while my baby plays, this never works out. It's all about getting as much done as possible in the evenings after he goes to sleep, and during those babysitter hours and his nap time. It's not easy to be a mom inventor while trying to be a mom too. It's my job to keep this baby safe and all the clothes washed and meals cooked and dishes clean.

I'll never understand why a mother who works at home and does the baby-raising job is considered to be not working. There are people who get paid to wash and cook and clean and do the same thing mothers (or nowadays some fathers) do for no pay. I learn to ask women whether they work outside the home instead of whether they work, as if being a stay-at-home mom is not working. It's a lot of work, people. You don't get time off for lunch or bathroom breaks. Keeping a little one entertained and happy and fed and clean and safe requires a ton of work. I start telling Eli that Dada is at his office rather than at work, because "at work" implies that I'm *not* at work.

We're off to The Huntington Gardens in Pasadena to take some photos for my PowerPoint presentation. Eli's wearing his nicest outfit, and he looks adorable. I clean his eyes with a wet cloth to make sure his goopy or crusty eye situation is handled. With my stroller, a blanket, and my prototypes, I sneak a photo shoot near some rosebushes. While Gary plays with our son, I make sure no one is around to see the prototypes or me photographing in an area where I have no permission to photograph. I grab a shot of Eli looking happy as he proudly holds Mama's great invention that he inspired. Then I stage a shot with his fingers in between the clip ends to show how this does not harm him. I am still amazed as I put the clip on his tiny fingers that this is truly a clip that is safe for babies to play with and yet can keep a blanket from falling off a stroller.

Eli is more interested in the fountain nearby than being a supermodel, so I put away the prototypes to ooh and aah over the koi fish instead. When we get home, I work out my million-dollar plan. My vision is to find an established baby-product company that will want to make blankyclips. They will pay royalties on their sales, and that will be that. Easy peasy. And with all the babies being born every day in the U.S., I figure I'll be seeing a nice return on my eventual investors' investment pretty quickly. My PowerPoint shows the market potential of blankyclips and says that "blankyclip fills a market void. Currently there's no product that attaches a blanket to a stroller. Over 4 million babies to be born in the U.S. this year. Toddlers up to 3 and 4 yrs. still use strollers as well. Therefore there are 16 million potential users and at $20 per package that would equal $320 million in the U.S. alone." $320 million!

After I put Eli to bed and kiss Gary good night, I head out to friends' homes with my presentation and my prototype. I've come up with a magic $25,000 figure to allow me to get the patent, trademark, and licensing deal. It's a big goal, but I want to ensure that I have enough money to make this really happen.

When I show the presentation to my mommy support group, they root me on every step of the way. One of these women, Abigail, is our resident computer graphics expert, so I happily turn to her for help in creating a logo. The fact that she's not trained in the exact department of creating a logo to market a product effectively doesn't mean too much at the time. More important is that she's part of my mommy support club, and that she's willing to help me for basically a bottle of red wine. The importance of wine for calming mommy nerves is a rich topic that I leave for someone else to write about.

Oh happy day! A friend says he will invest! He isn't sure which level of investing he's interested in, but he says that he believes in me and my idea. I'm so jazzed. The next day another friend jumps on board, and he hasn't even seen the presentation! He's investing in me, he tells me, and he figures whatever idea I have will be worth it. Then some married friends say they will invest at the highest level offered, $10,000. I'm blown away! It takes a lot of belief to write that kind of check, and I'm surprised, flattered, confident, and scared shitless all at the same time. Friends can be miraculous.

I don't always close the deal, though. Some friends encourage me but say no. I learn to get over it and keep going. I make a list of friends to reach out to after kiddie bedtime. I'm not crazy about asking friends for money, but at the same time I feel like they're going to be happy that I asked, because they'll soon be getting a nice return on their money because my idea is going to sell. How can it not? Enough with the black binder clips!

<hr>

It's easier to ask friends for money than to hand your anesthetized baby over to an eye surgeon. Turns out that the reason Eli's eye has been so crusty is that he has a tear duct that needs to be surgically opened up a bit more. I'm having extreme second thoughts about putting him through this—what kind of mother chooses surgery?—but now he's asleep and it's really too late to turn back. His surgery goes well, and when he wakes up he's cranky and crying, but I have never enjoyed holding a crying baby so much. We leave the surgical center relieved that all went well, but my nerves are beyond fried.

No time for wine, though, as I need to be at a friend's house by eight to show my presentation to her and her husband. At the kitchen table, she writes a check for $2,500 and becomes an investor because sometimes the universe understands what needs to happen at the end of a particularly challenging day.

This money-raising business keeps me busy. It stings a little when a friend asks, "Can we invest less than your lowest $2,500 option, because we won't mind losing less?" Ouch, no you cannot. But it doesn't matter because from all my pitches I raise the $25,000! I reach my goal. It's so exciting to open a bank account with all the money I'll need to turn my idea into a million-dollar business.

2

The Road to Licensing

In terms of what my next moves are, I decide maybe I should not buy a dress for my Oprah appearance just yet.

Now that I have the money in the bank, the next more important step is to get that patent. I call up the unsupportive attorney and tell her I'm ready to have her start writing me one. It's March 2005, and I am able to write her a check for her $2,500 retainer. Now she's mine! She then proceeds to tell me her fee: $485 per hour. It costs me $4 just to hear her say "$485 per hour"! After what must be an interminable pause, she suggests that her junior associate begin drafting my patent.

Gary leaves tonight on a business trip to China for his new job, which involves a huge daily commute to Orange County, but we have mouths to feed. So far his skills are proving way more marketable than mine, but he also feels strongly about being the provider for our little family. We are grateful that he landed this gig. Interesting how the model of working for one company and retiring from that same company (our parents' story) is a thing of the past. I can't imagine this will be the job he retires from.

After I put Eli to bed, I get busy doing more patent research. I keep searching through databases for patents that have similar elements. It's reassuring to look at patents for clips and strollers and even cribs, because it shows me my idea is not out there yet.

LIVING THE DREAM

In 2005, U.S. homeownership was at the highest level in history—about seven out of ten Americans had purchased homes. People who had never been able to afford to buy a house were given the tools to do so, even though housing prices were also at an all-time high. What could possibly go wrong?

It's June 2005, and I have no idea what's happening in the world of subprime mortgages and derivative trading (whatever the heck that is) and what it will mean to me. What I do know is that my utility patent application is finally and officially sent to the USPTO. Done and done. What a thrill it is to see my name on the top of the page next to the word *inventor*. I mean, isn't that what America is all about?

Then the law firm sends me their first bill: $9,086! Are you kidding me? I manage to talk my patent lawyer down to $5,489. Much better, but still. I'm now well aware that my $25,000 isn't going to last forever and stressed about how quickly hourly legal fees can accumulate. I'm so glad I applied for the trademark on my own.

When I try to buy the domain name for blankyclip, I'm told that it is taken. Huh? Someone has taken www.blankyclip.com? How can this possibly be? I search the web high and low (again!) to see if I missed something. Is there someone else out there who calls themself blankyclip? I can't find a company by that name other than mine, and there's no product out there by that name. All I can do is purchase a "backorder" for the domain name. This means that when it becomes available, I'll be contacted so I can purchase it. I'm a bit freaked out by this. I can't believe someone else owns www.blankyclip.com. Who has it and why? The name was available for me to grab the trademark. Why would someone have the domain name I need?

I tell myself that I'm making progress little by little. I mean, I've raised some capital, and my patent application is in progress, and I have a product name. If I equate my journey to a car trip from New York to Los Angeles, I feel like I'm somewhere around St. Louis. I'm blissfully unaware that I'm really stuck in traffic waiting to get to the Lincoln Tunnel to pull out of Manhattan.

All that patent research makes me very aware of baby products and what moms are digging out there in the world. I scan every stroller I see for accessories. Cup holders. Shopping bag holders. Cell phone holders. So many things we need to hold. And this is how I come across a product for babies and toddlers that I hadn't noticed before. It's a cup that holds snacks and has a special lid that lets the baby get to the snacks but also keeps the snacks—grapes or Cheerios or whatnot—from falling out. Its genius brand name is Snack Trap®.

I find the inventor of this product online and decide to call her for information. She's a mom and has invented a product that people are buying. What's the harm in calling and asking her for advice? I've always been good about cold-calling people. What feels like a lifetime ago, I was able to use this skill to get hold of casting directors or producers or agents who warned that they should never, under any circumstance whatsoever, be called by an actor. More recently, it's a skill that's helped me reach out to people and ask them to invest in my idea. I have a mantra that I repeat when I'm about to make a call that I'm feeling a bit hesitant to make. It goes like this: *In a hundred years we'll all be dead, so just make the call.* It takes a few days to reach her, but eventually I do. What I learn from this mom inventor is that she decided to manufacture her product on her own in the U.S., but manufacturing in China would cost me much, much less. China? It's an ordeal to get to the west side of LA, lady. I'm supposed to go to China?

During naptime (Eli's, not mine), I begin a new avenue of research.

I search for companies that are already manufacturing baby stroller accessories. Maybe one of them will be interested in making blankyclips and paying me royalties. I find a company called Kel-Gar, based in Texas. Kel-Gar makes a few baby items I like, including an inflatable tub that we used when Eli was a baby. The founder is interested in finding out more about my product. Sweet! Then I get through to an executive at another company, Kolcraft, and he wants to see a blankyclip, which is beyond exciting. I head to Kmart (so many Ks!) to check out Kolcraft strollers and research their products. I want to make sure that a blankyclip does indeed fit on their strollers. I pull out one of my prototypes and—yes!—it does. On all the stroller bars and handles and food trays. I'm excited about getting in to see this company.

If that isn't enough to make me feel great, Eli composes his first song. We sing it over and over again: "Butterfly, butterfly, shhhhh shhhhh." (Choreography: The pointer finger goes on the lips for the "shh" part.) Twenty months old and a songwriter! Gary and I are definitely ready to get pregnant again, but this old uterus is as quiet as one of Eli's shushed butterflies. So, the plan is to get me on the pill to lower my FSH (follicle stimulating hormone), which has climbed higher than we want it to be. Yes, I am taking the pill because I want to *get* pregnant. After even one month of taking the pill, a woman's FSH lowers, which increases her fertility. The second you get off the pill is when you are most likely to conceive. Maddening that most women don't know this. I hope it works for us.

September 2005. I now have meetings scheduled in Chicago with Kolcraft and in Dallas with Kel-Gar. So much to get ready for! I'm armed with a bunch of dangerous-for-babies clips that I'll contrast with a blankyclip. People use electrical pony clamps, black binder clips, clothespins, and food bag clips for lack of a better choice. Most of these clips are not only dangerous and unsightly but can't be attached to stroller tubing, stroller food trays, and sunshades. A blankyclip can! So, for my meetings, I ship these not-nice clips by Priority Mail directly to the hotel where I'm staying. This seems way easier than trying to bring them with me on the plane in my carry-on bag.

My meeting with the muckety-muck at Kolcraft goes well, but he's not interested in licensing my product. He explains that Kolcraft is mainly in the stroller and highchair business, selling items that will sit on the floor of a store, so he deals with the floor buyer. My product will be hanging on a peg, and Kolcraft doesn't work with buyers who deal with items that hang on pegs. What the heck? He tells me my product is terrific and will definitely do well, but they aren't the company to get it out there. I need to find a company that is already in the hanging-on-a-peg business and already has relationships with those buyers. It's all about the buyers, and there are specific buyers for every part of the store. He is incredibly supportive, though. He says he sees products all the time and this one is just great. But he does need to get going, so thank you so much for coming to see him.

I take my Ann Taylor Loft ass out of there and think about what I'm going to do with the rest of my afternoon. My flight back to Los Angeles is a few hours off, so I decide to enjoy a child-free stroll down Michigan Avenue. It's a beautiful sunny afternoon, and I'm on a business trip, and I am alone with no need to get anything done. Even with the disappointment at Kolcraft, I wish I had a hat I could throw up in the air like Mary Tyler Moore.

I arrive in Dallas a week later. My box of scary clips is waiting for me at the hotel. Such a business traveler I've become! With my carry-on for the one-night hotel stay and my business bag flung over my shoulder, you'd think I did this all the time. The trickiest part of traveling so far has been arranging babysitting help around the clock, or until my husband is home from ~~work~~ the office at night and after he leaves in the morning. It's expensive to pay someone else to do the mommying when I'm not around, but I've managed to get Zelma and Ada to cover the day between them from 7:00 a.m. to 6:00 p.m. With no family around, these women are my saviors. Eli is definitely not impressed by my ability to organize this schedule, but trust me, little guy, your mama is on a worthwhile mission!

I leave my hotel for the Kel-Gar meeting. In my rental, I drive never-ending highways and cloverleafs that roll back up onto more never-ending highways. I'm unsure of where I'm going, here in Dallas and here in my life. With every new highway and off-ramp, I question what I've done. What possessed me to invent a product anyway? Maybe that unsupportive patent attorney was right way back when— maybe my clip is just a clip and doesn't deserve all the effort I've been giving it. Then I find the building.

Kel-Gar has a stroller accessory in their line, so they are in that world of buyers. The founder and I have a conversation about licensing, and she's interested in blankyclip. But when she tells me how many units a year she sells of one of the products she manufactures, I'm not sure this is the right place for my product. Once I get into a licensing arrangement, I won't have any control over how well it sells. While she's explaining Kel-Gar's other products and access to buyers, I'm thinking about a five percent deal and my other investors. Suddenly it doesn't seem like I should be handing over my invention to a small company. A giant company that's selling millions of units is more what I had in mind. How do I get a meeting at one of those?

When I find a post office to ship back my box of scary clips, I meet a woman who has just moved to Dallas after being forced to leave New Orleans because of Hurricane Katrina which slammed into New Orleans at the end of August, less than two months ago. This woman had her world turned upside down and is starting over. Here I am trying to build a business based on a stroller accessory, and her life just fell apart. Humbling. Suddenly, a story in the news is a woman next to me, standing in line in the post office, putting my meeting with a small company into perspective.

Once again, I find myself with a few extra hours before my flight back to Los Angeles. It's a hot day, and there's no Michigan Avenue to walk down, so I end up at a mall. According to Wikipedia, Dallas has more stores and shopping centers per capita than any other U.S. city. The mall I end up in is the Galleria, and it's so big it has an ice skating rink in it! I answer my phone while I'm in a dressing room of a store I can't afford to shop in, and it's my dear friend Jessica from my mommy group. It feels so good to tell her about the meeting. I'm no longer anonymous in a city I have no ties to.

Whoops. I'm in complete shock when I return the rental car and discover I've missed my flight because I've read my itinerary wrong. It hits me that I'm maybe not as savvy as I'd like to believe I am. It's easy to break down into tears while talking to the Continental Airlines representative. These are tears about my missed flight, to be sure, but they are also tears born during the twenty months since I came up with the blankyclip idea, and these tears flow because of the things that have weighed on me since then—licensing, sales channels, utility patents, and business plans. The Continental rep takes pity and books me on a later flight at no charge.

Back home, I need to regroup. What am I really doing? Should I find a way to pay back my investors and end this? I'm exhausted, and I just don't know where to turn. So it is wonderful to receive a Notice of Publication from the USPTO. My trademark application has been accepted and processed. I now own blankyclip®. Yay! I thought when I applied that I would have the licensing deal all locked down by now, but I'll take this moment of happiness.

Then an opportunity comes up that is too good to refuse. Gary has a business trip in Hong Kong to talk to some factories for the golf club company he works for. He's arranged a meeting for me. The man I'm going to meet is a big honcho at a $7 billion company, and they make baby products. I'm not sure who's higher on the org chart—a big honcho or a muckety-muck—but my husband tells him about my product, and he's interested. I'm ecstatic.

Hong Kong isn't an overnight kind of trip, so we call in some backup. Nama (my mother) is flown in from New York to be with Eli for a week. Gary leaves first to have his meetings, and then I'm on a flight alone a few days later. It's about eighteen hours of flying with a change of planes in Taiwan. The airport in Taiwan is incredibly confusing. Where am I supposed to go to catch my next flight? No signs are in English. It's a miracle I find the right gate. When I finally arrive in Hong Kong, I find myself at a restaurant overlooking gorgeous Victoria Harbour. I am somehow at my husband's lunch meeting, trying to look human, but I'm delirious since I've been traveling for the past twenty-two hours.

Next morning, I can't believe I'm about to have my meeting at Li & Fung, the $7 billion company. Gary and I take a cab to the building, and I'm glad he's with me. We have the Li & Fung address written in Cantonese on a piece of paper that the cab driver reads. He could take us anywhere, and what would we do? I stick out like a sore thumb with my blond curly hair, and it feels bizarre to see signs that I can't decipher and nothing that is familiar. At the building, we take the elevator up to the office, stopping on several floors. Everybody who gets on or off the elevator seems really young, some of them wear lab coats, and there's a busy but friendly atmosphere. We don't have to wait long to meet with Oliver, a tall white-haired Dutchman.

Oliver is excited about my product. He makes jokes about how many millions of dollars we're going to make together selling it. My head spins. He tells me that his company owns Toys "R" Us in Asia. They also own Circle K Stores, the small convenience stores. He sees my product selling in grocery stores, as that's where women shop with strollers and where baby accessories are sold in Asia. He'll start by talking to the buyers he works with in the grocery business. We're shaking hands and saying good-bye less than thirty minutes after we meet. I'm not so much walking out of his office as floating out.

Gary and I decide to celebrate such an amazing meeting with afternoon tea at the Peninsula Hotel. We are beyond thrilled. The hotel is incredibly elegant and looks like something right out of a fairy-tale movie. What a perfect way to end this trip—so full of promise and optimism. Oliver actually said we are going to make millions! Now we can fly home.

3

Manufacturing a Clip and a Customer

November 2005. One week after we land, Oliver's no longer on board.

The bubble bursts when he shows my prototype to his supermarket buyers and they're not interested. And that's that. I'm devastated. The power these buyers wield! But Oliver does say that if I'd like him to manufacture my product, he would be happy to send a quote. Thank goodness it was only a fancy tea that I splurged on back in Hong Kong. Well, and maybe a pair of cute earrings from the subway station underground mall.

So, I'm back to calling baby product manufacturers about licensing. I'm feeling hopeless about getting these companies interested in my idea when Oliver emails me information about the nuts and bolts of manufacturing. His company would find me a factory, and my minimum order would be for 10,000 blankyclips. I would need to take care of product testing. Should this information be making me so uneasy?

It is a happy day, though, as my ovulation kit tells me that I am at three bars! I might not know how to make a blankyclip today, but I know how to make us a baby. Don't I?

Actually, I don't seem to know how to make a baby either. Being on the pill did lower my FSH, and yet I did not get pregnant after I stopped taking it, so this month we're trying a round of Clomid, a drug used for the treatment of infertility. I am taking this pill for five days in hopes that it increases my chance of getting pregnant by increasing the number of follicles developing in my ovaries and therefore the number of eggs releasing. I know, very, very sexy.

An important email from the USPTO informs me that in order to officially use blankyclip®, I need to be "using the mark in commerce"—that is, selling blankyclips. Since I'm not doing that yet, I need to file an Extension Request. Five months ago, when I thought I could start using the ®, I was wrong. The Extension Request buys me six months, and they'll grant me five more of these before I have to be actually selling blankyclips.

When my phone rings, it is not a call from a baby product company wanting to license my blankyclip idea, but it leaves me stunned nonetheless. A toddler program has a spot that just opened up, and do I want to grab it for Eli? Getting a spot in any kind of program for toddlers is a miracle in Los Angeles. This one is a transition program for kids who are too young for preschool. Eli has been going with me on school tours for next year, when he'll be of age for most preschools. He cries when it's time to leave because he wants to stay and be a part of whatever's going on in whatever school we're checking out. If I take this Monday/Wednesday/Friday morning spot for him, it will give me more time to work on becoming a baby product manufacturer, which seems to be my next step. How is it that the boy who was two months old when I picked up his dirty blanket and came up with the idea for a baby-safe blanket clip is now two years old?

Eli is excited about going to "school." He has absolutely no anxiety about my leaving him there. I'm the one with the anxiety. In the first few minutes of his very first day, he comes up to me in his new classroom and says, "Bye, Mama!" With a big smile he toddles off to be with his new classmates, and the teacher nods for me to take my cue and go. And what a twist: I'm the one crying. How can he be so fine about being left in a new environment without me? What have I done wrong? Couldn't he have suffered just a teensy bit?

So now I have three mornings a week to devote to blankyclip. I hunker down in this brave new world. I'm going to manufacture and distribute my invention on my own. Eli's not the only one taking baby steps. I sing, "The wipers on the bus go swish, swish, swish, and I need a factory to make blankyclips." Easy to see why the mommy on the bus might want a drink, drink, drink. I am so far out of my comfort zone that I couldn't see it with a telescope.

Comfortable or not, I reach out to Oliver in China and ask for some quotes. I am pretty anxious about it all. Oliver tells me about the cost of tooling, which is the mold they'll need to create to manufacture the inner plastic clip ($4,000–$10,000), the clips ($1.16 per piece), his company's commission (five percent), and testing costs (are you getting sleepy?). He requests artwork for the blister card, which is part of the packaging. It will take about three months before they can ship a manufactured, packaged blankyclip.

January 25, 2006. My first late-night call with Kelvin from Li & Fung in Hong Kong. I've only been dealing with Oliver up to this point, but he's handed me off to an assistant. Because of the time change, we have to start the call at 10:30 p.m. my time in LA, which is 1:30 p.m. the next day in Hong Kong. With my son and husband both sound asleep, Kelvin and I discuss packaging issues and options. We discuss making the mold for my clip. I have about a zillion questions for him, and one for myself: Is a theater major actually discussing manufacturing blankyclips in China?

It's going to be necessary for me to incorporate and form a company if I'm going to manufacture and sell a product. I meet with our accountant, Judy, who asks me about my cash flow needs, picking a DBA ("Doing Business As" name), whether I'll be a sole proprietorship, and if I have investors and a business plan. I'm sure I look like a deer in the headlights, but I did not learn these things in Method acting class.

I'm so glad for the Krispy Kreme located next door to a Babies "R" Us. Instead of doing more product research, I need to drown my sorrows in a doughnut. Jessica, my bestest partner-in-crime mommy friend, tells me she is moving away to San Jose. I'm crushed. Since having our babies, we have seen each other nearly every day. She has seen me through the pain of nursing with Eli's "immature suck" and the joy of everyday nothingness. We've laughed and cried about becoming mothers and giving up creative pursuits. Our children have been the best of buddies. How I wish she did not know the way to San Jose.

⁂

February 2006. With every email I get from Kelvin, I have ten more questions. Now I realize that I don't want a blister pack for the packaging. That'll be too hard and won't let the customer get a feel for the clips. I need a header card and a polybag instead. I want there to be one clip per bag. And I have to find out what warning statements need to be on my packaging. Most importantly, the clip tension needs to match my prototype. And, on second thought, let's go with two clips per bag. Makes more sense, as they really need two clips to do the job right, one for the top and one for the bottom of the stroller.

It's getting me a little crazy trying to deal with all these manufacturing questions over email and late-night phone calls, so I'm intrigued when a friend suggests that I call these other guys in the manufacturing world who might be able to help me get my product made—and who have an office in Los Angeles. They are Orthodox Jews who manufacture toys for fast food chains, pens for hotels, and other odd little items. They work in an office that's in complete disarray, but their company is worth a fortune.

When we meet in their conference room, they ask me to forgive the mess—empty Coke cans and food wrappers everywhere. The guys are young and wearing white button-down shirts. I feel like I'm in lower Manhattan, hearing their quick singsongy speech. They're surprisingly nice to me, and they really like my product. The thought of working with someone in Los Angeles, in my own time zone, beats the heck out of late-night phone calls to Hong Kong. Judging by all the Happy Meal insert toys and M&M brand toys, I quickly conclude that they are the real deal. Then I see a collection of plush toys that they've sourced from China. I pick up a teddy bear that's sitting on top of a tube full of candy.

"Maybe we could stick a stuffed animal on a blankyclip," I joke.

The room falls silent.

It's what everybody who doesn't know what to get an expecting mother buys her: a teddy bear! So, we could make a plush toy that doubles as a blanket clip. The Orthodox guys want me to leave both a finished prototype and an extra inner plastic clip that hasn't been covered with padding and fabric. They like the plush toy-blankyclip idea and say they can work up some samples of a few different animal options. This could be a game changer.

On the pregnant front, I am scoring a big fat zero. After being on the pill to lower my FSH, taking a round of Clomid, and even trying acupuncture, we are now in the hands of a fertility doctor to see how to bump it up, so to speak. As I'm approaching forty, time is of the essence. A day after seeing the fertility doctor, a nurse is giving me shots of Menopur in my abdomen to increase the number of eggs that will enter the Who Gets Fertilized contest. She shows my husband how to do it so he can take give me the remaining shots for the week, sparing me all those office visits. I'm in the lucky group of women who have already had a child but now need some extra support to get pregnant again. The doctor assures me that the shots and a dash of artificial insemination will do the trick. I'm also in the even luckier group of women who have a father who is able and willing to pay for this intervention. Gary and I don't have the $4,000 these drugs and doctor visits will cost us. The pang for a sibling for Eli is so deep that seeing a pregnant woman makes my heart ache these days. My eyes are tearing up with gratitude as I thank my father over the phone. "This means so much to me," I tell him.

"Now will you stop all this blankyclip nonsense?"

After eight days of shots in my abdomen and three ultrasounds, today is the big day. Gary and I both need to attend this appointment, as he has to give a "specimen." Seems like a huge disconnect that I am trying to create a human being to love and protect, and Gary is being handed a cup and a DVD to watch. While the specimen is being "prepared," I change into a gown. Without question, my end of the bargain involves no pleasure and a certain degree of discomfort as a fine catheter is inserted through my cervix into my uterus to directly deposit Gary's sperm. I lie there for about fifteen minutes imagining that one of my nudged-along eggs has met her match and our little family will soon grow. I get dressed, and we go to pick Eli up from school. No one is the wiser as we continue the day with lunch, a park play date, and Eli's swim class.

CLIPPED

March 2006. The State of California officially incorporates The blankyclip Company. My idea—conceived over two years ago—is legally recognized! And speaking of conceiving, I am pregnant! See what a little romance (surprisingly little), and some hormone shots followed by insemination can do for a girl? The pregnancy pee stick is a bit vague about announcing that I am indeed pregnant on this twenty-ninth day of my cycle, but the blood test from the fertility clinic is not. It worked! Eli will not be an only child.

The Orthodox guys call to tell me that the plush-toy blankyclip samples have arrived from China. The factory added an animal character—a duck, a pig, a frog, a bear, and a sheep—on the top of the clips, which makes them double as toys, and they're wonderful. Now my product looks less like a clip and more like a stuffed animal.

It's at this moment that blankyclip transforms from its original design into a "plush toy that doubles as a baby-safe clip." The animals need a little work, but we can see that with some minor fixes they're going to be great. It's crazy to me that I'm holding my product, produced by a factory in China. It looks like a real friggin' product! I have to pay $1,050 for these samples, but I'm excited about their evolution. We haven't discussed pricing with the factory, but for a first attempt, they've done a terrific job. My Orthodox guys announce that they want to move forward. They believe in my product and see it doing very well. I'm stoked!

During one of my lifesaving playdate sessions with my mommy group, we are discussing how I'll sell the animal blankyclips, when I have an idea. What if I include a blanket with two blankyclips and sell them as a gift set? The moms seem to agree that this is a nice way to merchandise my product. I mean, the clips are meant to hold a blanket, and adding the blanket makes for a great baby gift. It also allows me to raise my price point, which works out if I can find an affordable blanket. Amazing what good ideas can be hatched while sitting cross-legged on a foam floor mat decorated with the ABCs.

It's been a while since I corresponded with the Li & Fung folks, as I didn't put in an order with them for blankyclips. I reach out to ask about blankets, and all the emails bounce. So, I email my buddy Oliver, the head guy at Li & Fung who was so excited about all the millions we were going to make, and I ask him about blankets. He puts me in touch with a new contact, Heather, and she sends me a quote for a solid fleece blanket, $1.35. That sounds like an excellent number, but how would I pay for 5,000 of these suckers?

I meet with my Orthodox guys. They say they will handle the development and design of the product. The financing. The insurance. The importation/duty/housing of the product. And the sales team. They are not good at going to trade shows, small stores, or big stores. They are good at putting together a sales team. Until I can get a credit line, they will fund the orders. Wow, this is fantastic! But then I have to pay them back. And for this they want fifty percent of my company. Wait, what?

We talk about the ABC Kids Expo, the big trade show that is coming up, sponsored by the JPMA (Juvenile Products Manufacturers Association). The guys tell me that all I need to do is be there with the prototype to take orders, and then we'll manufacture based on the orders we receive. I'm unsure of this strategy. I don't have packaging, I don't have any printed marketing materials, and I don't feel at all ready to be at a trade show. They assure me that this is how it's done. The trade show is two months away. Somehow, I agree to sign up to be an exhibitor.

I drive home from our meeting with more doubt than enthusiasm. I'm not sure about so much. Did I mention that they're asking for fifty percent of my company? Half of blankyclip! And they expect to get paid for the merchandise once the orders have come in, which basically means they're putting up the money for me to manufacture in exchange for fifty percent. This won't be a workable deal, especially as I'm a new company that will need more capital—and the only means I'll have to raise capital will be with shares of my company. I'll need to maintain at least a fifty-one percent controlling interest and leave myself room to bring others in.

The most I can offer the guys is twenty-five percent ownership, but they need to agree to cover the cost of that first production run as well. And if their price is not competitive, or my quality standards are not met, or they fail to meet delivery schedules, then I can end the relationship. I'm building a company, and so I need to hold aside ten percent for employees. Stock is what will keep people in the company. I've got to remember that I have the upper hand, as this is my invention. I am woman, hear me roar!

As I'm driving over to negotiate with my Orthodox guys once again, I'm so nauseous from being pregnant that I have to pull over to the side of the road and vomit onto Santa Monica Boulevard. I'm glad I have some water in the car to wash my mouth out, and some minty gum. Within minutes, I'm at the Orthodox guys' office, and I'm giving them my terms. They're not happy, and even tell me that they have their doubts about partnering with a woman who could go off and get pregnant, and then where would that leave them and the business? I decide to keep quiet about the fact that I have actually had a lovely prego incident only moments ago. I just vomited on the street, and yet I'm here at this meeting because I am committed to making this happen, and these guys are telling me they don't know about partnering with a woman? Because I could get pregnant? Such chauvinism is beyond maddening.

But instead of going off on a Women Who Run With the Wolves tirade to enlighten these men on the innate power of women and our ageless knowing, I sit there and discuss tooling and warehousing, packaging, testing, and freight. I'm feeling quite amazed with myself and how far I've come since I first heard that Snack-Trap® inventor suggest I manufacture in China. After many long phone calls with a friend who is an expert at business building, I offer twenty-five percent of my company to my Orthodox guys. "We'll think about it, but what we had in mind was fifty percent," one of them tells me. Even without an MBA, I know this is ridiculous.

Within days, I hear back that they now have manufacturing quotes from China. They can get two blankyclips made for $5.50. My market research tells me that I can sell two blankyclips for $17, so that seems perfect. But here's why it actually is not perfect and why this will not work at all: If $17 is the retail price for a set of blankyclips, then the wholesale price (what I will actually be getting) is $8.50 or even less. A $3 profit means that if I sell 5,000 of these pairs I'll make a whopping $15,000, but then there's the cost of making the mold (about $6,000) and doing the safety testing (another $5,000), which leaves me with $4,000 to cover all the expenses of running this business. Even more shocking is that after I have sold all these incredible blankyclips I will have absolutely zero to pay for a reorder.

Which is why their scenario of covering the cost of manufacturing the first order but then requiring me to pay them back in full in exchange for fifty percent of my business is a fantasy. How about I offer you guys five percent because I'm going to need the remaining shares to raise investment and make this a viable company?

They take a look at the well-thought-out and most businesslike email I've ever written. And they say no. If they can't get fifty percent, they want nothing. They won't front any of my manufacturing costs. They'll be contract manufacturers for me, and that's it. So, I no longer have a partner, but I have a factory. As long as I pay for the order.

<hr />

May 2006. Our home is filled with good cheer as Eli has his milestone first poop in the potty. We dance and celebrate as if he's done the impossible. But that's not the only poopy news in my life. Ruth, the USPTO examiner of my utility patent application, informs me that she isn't sure what a child-safe fastening device is supposed to be or do, or how it's different from all the other clips in the world. Is that all? My patent attorney suggests we send professional drawings of blankyclip in action. What's another $450? We shoot those over to Ruth and cross our fingers. So much is riding on her decision to grant me this patent.

Gary comes home from work with exciting news. He has a potential investor for me, a guy named Sal, who's in the cardboard business. He met with Gary about that business, and somehow blankyclip came up, and now he wants to meet with me. I need to put together some revised documents that show why he should invest and how much money I need in order to start manufacturing. This time around, I'm asking for $80,000, a sum that should cover my manufacturing costs and allow me to market blankyclips once they arrive from China.

In another era, Sal and I might have met in his family's Sicilian restaurant in Little Italy, and he may have said something like, "I'm gonna make you an offer you can't refuse." In this era, we meet in a Macaroni Grill. His silk shirt is opened three buttons down, and he steps out of a sports car that probably costs more than the house I grew up in. He barely looks over the documents I've spent hours and hours putting together, he's investing in me, not the product. He likes how passionate I am about blankyclip, and he tells me, "I have an especially good feeling about your business." Sal doesn't seem to care much what a blankyclip is. He says that this investment of $80,000 really means nothing to him, nor does he need it back. He's just happy that he can help me move forward with my vision. I try hard to play it cool with this information. He's about to change my life, and I'm ecstatic.

Sal wants a timeline for my expenditures, and he wants to go over the "nitty-gritty" of the business relationship and what it will entail. We discuss the manufacturing process and what I need the capital for. In return for his investment, he wants ten percent of blankyclip. Down the line, we'll need to bring in a senior salesperson and other staff, so shares of the company need to be held for those positions. I am getting really good at this.

I notice that a check to make my dreams come true does not arrive, so I call Sal to ask for the letter of intent—the letter that states how much he's willing to invest in my company. He confirms that he's in for $80,000 and ten percent of my company. Nice! He wants to talk more tomorrow about the details.

I call him in the morning after I imagine he's had a few espressos, and Sal officially bails.

The "details" he wants to talk about include having him run my business. He wants to handle my books, and he wants all things related to money to go through his business—his accountant, his everything. In other words, he doesn't want to invest in my company, he wants complete control. Who knows what he'll run through my books? I say that I can't agree to his terms, and he tells me he's out.

So much for wanting to support someone with a dream! One minute I'm about to have the investment I need to begin manufacturing, and the next I'm back to bupkis.

July 2006. The USPTO sends me a Notice of Approval for my trademark Extension Request. All I have to do is send another check for $150, and I can hold my trademark for six more months while I work to "use the mark in commerce." It's not much money, but it's somehow enough to trigger my financial concerns. I'm pregnant and living in an apartment, which doesn't feel like the right place for me to be raising my family in Los Angeles. My husband needs a better-paying job that isn't sixty miles away, and I would like to not describe my marriage as "strained." I would like to have a yard for my son to play in and for him to invite his friends over to play in this very same yard. It's summertime, and he's supposed to be frolicking in a kiddie pool outside, not stuck inside our apartment.

My family starts attending three-year-old birthday parties for the kids in Eli's transition to preschool class. At Sophie's birthday party, I meet one of the dads, Ethan. We start talking, and when I tell him about blankyclip, he matter-of-factly says that he knows a woman he'd love to connect me with. "She has your same bubbly zest and passion for projects!" he tells me enthusiastically.

She differs from me in that she has a lot of money and is able to invest in cool adventures. Ethan knows this woman, Linda, from his filmmaking life, as she invested in a movie he was part of. Anyone who invests in movies has money to burn, so I'm eager to meet her. He tells me that she's super busy and works in real estate.

Two weeks later, I'm on the one-hour flight to San Jose, California, to meet Linda. Over the phone, I made it seem real cazh, and that it's no problem to meet for coffee even though I live in LA, am pregnant, and have a toddler. She certainly isn't going to come to me, so I'm more than willing to fly up to see her. I'm so glad she's squeezed in a coffee meeting for me.

We meet at her real estate office in an upscale suburb of San Jose. She shows me all the real estate awards she's won, prominently displayed in her office, and then we head out to a coffee shop down the street. I show her the presentation I've put together, which basically asks for a $300,000 investment in exchange for ten percent of the company.

"It's amazing how you've invented a product and are getting it made. I've had so many ideas for products, but I've never gotten as far as you have," she offers. She's supportive, sweet, and gracious, but gives me her bottom line: "I'm just not in a position to invest right now." Did I have to fly to San Jose for a cup of coffee? We have coffee in Los Angeles.

The investment figure I am seeking is now up to $300,000 because I did some math. The math entailed my adding up the cost of manufacturing 10,000 blankyclips, buying 5,000 blankets, safety testing, tooling, package design, insurance, patents, trade shows, an accountant, and warehousing. Then there's advertising, PR, marketing, incidentals, R&D, and office supplies. A big problem is that the profit margin has to pay for the next production order, which will probably cost more than the first—because I'll be ordering more to sell more!

Another sign of how long I've been trying to get this business going is that we're now looking for a big-boy bed for Eli. The missy that's growing in my belly has dibs on his crib. The bed we check out from a posting on Craigslist is scratched up and covered in crayon marks. My son will spend many hours of his life attached to this piece of furniture, and these people think it's okay to leave its previous tenant's crayon streaks all over it? I'm disgusted, and my mood is getting dark. It could be all the hormones raging in my pregnant body, or it could be that this world has become so friggin' expensive.

I want my son's first bed to be clean and new, so we find ourselves inside Babystyle. I'm interested in seeing what kind of products they carry and where mine might fit. It's an upscale baby boutique kind of store, full of mostly baby clothes and maternity wear, but I'm imagining blankyclips in there soon. I'm kind of amazed to see that the place is a mess and disorganized, and the staff doesn't seem too involved in selling. The plush items are a bit dirty, and it worries me that my blanket and clips could get dirty if they're displayed in the same way. Gary can see this isn't helping my state of mind and lovingly says, "Let's go grab some ice cream."

When I was pregnant with Eli, I took Bradley birthing classes with a woman, Beth, who now owns a baby boutique. We meet so I can show her my product and discuss the animal options I've got so far. She helps me choose which designs of blankyclip animals to manufacture first. We pick one that would target girls, one for boys, and one for "we don't know what's coming." The blankets packaged with each design would follow suit. We decide that the brown bear and a blue blanket would work for boys, the yellow duck and an ecru blanket for the unisex version, and the white sheep and a pink blanket for girls. Beth tells me that because the sheep has a spot of pink in the ear it can and will only be sold for girl babies. There must not be even a stitch of pink for an animal meant for a boy baby. This isn't what she thinks is right; it's what she's seen in her customers' purchases. I'm surprised since we're talking about a sheep, which seems like it could just as easily be an animal a boy would like. Beth further warns me that if a stuffed animal has a pink nose it is branded as female, and I should be careful about little details like that. This is great market research and certainly eye-opening to see how narrowly we define boys and girls while still in their swaddles!

It's reassuring to hear that Beth loves my product and thinks it'll be a great baby gift. She shows it to her employees, and they all tell me how cute it is. This gives me the impetus to head to one of my favorite dreamy baby stores, the Juvenile Shop, to show the woman who does their buying how my blankyclips have been progressing. She saw my original prototypes long ago and is happy with the design change of adding a plush animal. She recognizes me as an occasional customer, so that helps. "These will sell," she says in almost a menacing tone. She's not warm with me like Beth was, but I love this shop. It's incredibly busy, carries amazing products, and caters to a high-end clientele. I'll keep showing up here, although I do get incredibly nervous each time I talk to the buyer. I shouldn't take it personally that she's got a tough-girl act, but I do. It's helpful to be creating relationships with these buyers and getting their feedback that I am on the right track. But more importantly, to hear that they will want to someday put in orders!

There's another upscale baby boutique called Spirituali in my neighborhood, and I decide to pop in on that one as well. I show a saleswoman my three designs. She's encouraging and says she thinks they would do great in the store, but she never really knows what the owner/buyer, Myriam, will like, and it's all up to her. I have learned that the buyer is a person both revered and feared in a store, and when the buyer is the owner, I can only imagine the power that combo yields. Buyers make me revert to my elementary schoolgirl self who feels insecure and powerless. But I get Myriam's email info nonetheless because, confident or not, I must march on!

It's hot, and I'm gaining a lot of weight with this pregnancy. Having a toddler to take care of and a business to grow means I have to get creative about sneaking a quick nap when exhaustion takes over. It feels wrong, but I let Eli watch TV today while I proceed to pass out on the sofa. "Mommy just needs to close her eyes," I tell him, and the sweet little bunny Miffy, from his favorite show, is my salvation.

August 2006. I meet with Diane, the buyer for the baby store chain Right Start. It has thirty stores in the U.S., so this is a biggie. Her office is in Calabasas, twenty miles down the road from me. My six-month-pregnant belly is hanging out between us, but we don't even mention it. She seems to honestly love blankyclip. "But our store isn't where you'll start selling your product," she says.

What the heck?

Diane explains, "Your first step will be to get into the smaller baby boutiques. That's where your product will start to get noticed and build awareness. Once it has sold in that environment and proven it's an item people want, then it will be time to bring it into our stores." She adds, "I love that blankyclip was invented by a mom who saw a need for a product that wasn't already out there." She's so nice that I can't believe how easy this meeting is. She's practically selling the product to me! This is a really good sign, I think. I can't wait to get blankyclips into boutiques to build awareness.

I've seen other products travel this same path, where at first they're only in small stores and then one day I see them at Right Start or Babies "R" Us. I'm thinking of Boppy pillows, Robeez shoes, Baby Einstein videos, Skip Hop diaper bags, and on and on. The big stores don't want to experiment with a product—they let the smaller stores do that. It's much less of a risk for the boutiques, which buy in small quantities. It will take hard work to get into the boutiques, store by store. I've been hoping things would happen much faster. But the good news is that I have made an amazing contact, and she has basically said she will carry my product once it's established in the boutique world.

On the big-boy bed front, we find a beautiful bed for Eli at Wickes Furniture for $800. They have this great installment plan that lets us make payments for eighteen months with no interest. Not that we're thrilled to have more debt, but Eli will be sleeping in it for many years. It is the bed we will have memories of, and I want it to be a bed we love. Thank goodness for payment plans and stores that can part with merchandise before they get paid in full.

September 2006. Gary and I are celebrating his birthday, our tenth wedding anniversary, and the last chance for a weekend away before becoming parents of two. We fly to New York so my family can watch Eli, and then we slip away to Nova Scotia for a babymoon. We enjoy dining out and seeing a movie and eating Canadian chocolate. We do not enjoy thinking about our finances, our desire to move out of our apartment, and how in the world I am going to survive having a toddler, a newborn, and a new business while my husband commutes 120 miles round trip every day to his office and is not around to help me.

It ain't easy for any of my mama friends. If we stay at home while our husbands work outside the home, we think we should be doing more with our lives, and if we go back to the jobs we had before the baby, we think we aren't with our baby enough. My friend who teaches at a university is in pain about not being at home with her son. So, our mommy group continues to meet because this is where we go to unload and commiserate.

I get a call from my patent lawyer, who tells me she's leaving the firm. I've never had a lawyer leave me before, but I'm sad that it's over between us. She was unsupportive, sure, but always professional; she gave me good advice, and she was the first person I spoke with about my invention. Soon after, I get a call from the $330 per hour junior associate who's now handling my patent full-time. The junior attorney tells me that he too is leaving the firm, and that the firm is actually folding. Folding? I've never heard of such a thing—a business that's so entrenched and established closing up shop—but I'm about to get more experience there. It's nearing the end of 2006, and for now the stock markets are bullish. And even though there's some NPR buzz about some kind of mortgage crisis, I don't know how that matters. I mean, we rent our apartment.

So off I go to meet with a new lawyer, Henry, and we hit it off. He has his own firm and is definitely interested in working with me on the patent. It's a whole different story from dealing with the previous law firm, which had lots of bigger fish to fry than me. I tell Henry that Ruth, the USPTO examiner, has an issue with my application that I will call "the clip-on earring conflict." Seriously, the examiner does not see how my invention differs from a clip-on earring. Henry reworks the language on my application and files an amendment. "I wasn't expecting an amendment to cost so much, and I'm really hoping you can help me out with this $2,700 invoice," I tell him on the day it arrives. Thankfully the $2,700 bill drops to $2,100. Gary tells me this is a skill I should be proud of. I don't think of it as a skill. It's more of a survival mechanism.

4

A Baby, A Bank Loan, and Brownies

November 2, 2006. We are ten days away from my due date, and we get a big surprise at my OB visit. This active baby who has been enjoying moving around in my belly like nobody's business has found herself in a breech position. After an entire pregnancy with her head down, she now has her legs where her head should be. For this to occur so late in the pregnancy, when technically I could have the baby at any moment, is something that has made even my doctor's head spin. She says she didn't think it was possible for a baby to go breech this late in the game.

I head to an acupuncturist—I love my OB for suggesting this—to see what some needles can do to get this baby to turn back around. A breech baby means a cesarean birth, and I'm hoping to avoid that. As I'm now fifty-six pounds heavier than when my husband gave me that first shot to my abdomen, I can barely see my feet or the needles that have been inserted in my pinky toes. A gentle man burns a sage stick next to the needles for added influence. Somehow this is designed to get the baby back to her head-down vaginal-delivery-ready position.

Afterwards we head to our favorite Japanese restaurant for some sushi (naughty raw fish!) and a Diet Coke (evil caffeine!). This is not a suggestion from my doctor, but if the baby is going to play dirty, then I can too. I've been clean for nine months of both my addictions, and now I say enough is enough. You have brought me to my knees, darling.

Next morning, I call the hospital to discuss my appointment to have a "version," a procedure also recommended by my OB in which a doctor will attempt to nudge the baby into flipping over. Not a pleasant experience, I've heard, but my last chance to avoid a C-section. When the hospital informs me that I cannot have this procedure because there are no beds available, I let out a giant cry. Gary suggests we head back to my OB to see if the acupuncture has possibly worked, as the baby has certainly been moving a lot. Lo and behold, she has indeed put herself back in the head-down position, and we are back in business for a natural delivery. My doctor says, "I've never known a baby to do this in the thirty-ninth week of a pregnancy, and if I hadn't seen it on my own monitor with my own eyes, I would not have thought it was possible." My girl is already doing the impossible.

November 22, 2006. Our baby daughter is born! We name her Dagny, after the powerful, brilliant, and unstoppable protagonist in the book *Atlas Shrugged*. I'll do my best to keep moving forward with blankyclip, but the reality is that I have a new baby in the house. I'm so grateful she's here and she's healthy. Now I have even more motivation to make this company work. I want her to be proud of her mommy when she grows up. I can't wait to get blankyclip out into the world. I also can't wait to get past this stage of life, where I can watch my three-year-old pee in his pants because he didn't make it to the potty, then notice the pee run out of his pant leg onto the carpeted floor, and I can't do anything about it because my newborn is attached to my boob—the real kind—and I can't move from the very specific position I am in on my nursing chair. Oy!

January 2007. The universe sends me a baby gift. Out of the clear blue, GoDaddy informs me that blankyclip.com is now available. I buy the domain name and their private registration service, so my info is not out there for anyone to see. What a relief to finally own the domain for blankyclip! How odd that no one ever responded when I tried to reach out to find out who was holding it, and that no one ever contacted me to try to sell it to me.

I find a graphic designer, Patty, by calling the Otis Design School. We meet at a coffee shop nearby, and she shows me her portfolio. I love her work and the calm manner she shares it with me. She shows me a range of styles, and I feel like she's the right person to work with. She's really young, just out of school, but has a surprisingly mature way about her. This is my first face-to-face blankyclip meeting since having my baby. Thank goodness for nursing pads to prevent the wet booby look, because timing a meeting with a baby's needs falls in the realm of impossible. My breasts, in their special way, let me know that this fun meeting is over and it's time to rush home and feed Dagny.

SUBPRIME TIME

A brief recession in December 2001 triggered the U.S. Federal Reserve to drop its lending rate to near record lows—all the way down to 1.75%. Suddenly, bankers had lots of cheap money to play with, and they figured they could use this cash to help people who did not necessarily have the means to buy homes, because, well, bankers are such good-hearted folks. Lots of homes were sold in the next few years. To lots of people who couldn't really afford them. But subprime mortgages made them *think* they could afford them. And the bankers who extended those subprime mortgages could then just sell them to other banks. And everyone was happy! Except the twenty-five subprime lenders who filed for bankruptcy in early 2007. Turned out that when the interest rates started to rise, those people who couldn't afford their homes— well, they stopped paying for them. But twenty-five bankrupt subprime lenders out of the hundreds and hundreds who were doing the lending wasn't really a cause for concern. Then.

April 2007. Ruth, the USPTO examiner, writes that she's still not sure she understands what a blankyclip is or why it deserves a utility patent. She's not denying the patent application just yet, she just wants more clarity (beyond the thirty-two-page application and dozen drawings). To clear up Ruth's confusion, we send her some marketing photos I took showing blankyclip in use. I get a call from Henry, my new lawyer, saying that Ruth likes the photos. This is excellent news. I'm feeling good about working with Henry and Patty. I'm assembling a great team! Henry works on some further amendments to send to Ruth, to help clarify and expand upon the claims I'm making on my application.

But having a team means there are now people behind this product, and they are counting on me to deliver. This is why I'm showing a PowerPoint presentation to a couple who seem to have lots of cash. We are now living in the ground-floor apartment of a duplex (moving up in the world—we have a little yard!) in a part of town that's filled with gorgeous homes. These are new friends from my son's preschool nearby. The husband is a hedge fund manager.

The wife is a big blankyclip fan and really wants her husband to come on board. I show them the presentation on their front porch while kids are going crazy all around us. My husband is holding our new baby, but there are three other toddlers who are most intrigued by the computer and my slides. When they are finally off and running, we're able to have a more adult conversation. The hedge fund dad tells me, "I like to invest in companies that are already holding big orders from stores like Target, because then I know I'll make back my money. It doesn't make any sense for me to take such a risk with you."

Really, Mr. Hedge Fund? I keep reminding myself of that great Wallace Stevens line: "After the final no there comes a yes / And on that yes the future world depends."

July 2007. What about Citibank? I've been a loyal customer there for years now. Couldn't they give me a line of credit? Apparently, no. I ask the guy I see every time I come in to do my banking, "Can we discuss a line of credit?"

He flatly explains, "We only give money to businesses that have been operating for two years." He holds up two fingers to make sure I really get it. All my years of being a loyal customer and the fact that I deposited my $25,000 investment here are getting me zilch.

Adrienne Alitowski, President, The blankyclip Company, Inc. The first time I see those words on my brand-spanking-new business cards, my eyes well up. I've been at this for three and a half years—raised money, filed for patents, vomited in the street, and traveled to the other side of the world—and gazing upon my business card is one of those moments that stands out, that makes this marathon feel winnable. A business card. Something to hold on to. Something to hand to the person across the conference table that legitimizes me, that announces who I am. And who I am is a woman ... a mother ... with a business card. I pluck one out of the box. It feels like it was printed on a gum wrapper. These are the flimsiest business cards I've ever encountered. I don't know if I can realistically call them "cards." Patty, who ordered them for me online, is horrified. She's going to send them back. It's amazing how many things have to be done over and over again to get them right.

UP, UP, AND AWAY

July 19, 2007. The Dow Jones Industrial Average closed up 82.19 points at 14,000.41. It was the first time in history that the DJIA closed above 14,000 points. Charcoal-suited men snapped their suspenders and pumped handshakes in celebration. The good times were here to stay!

August 2007. Is it terrible that I'm thinking of my daughter's eight-month appointment with her pediatrician as a fantastic investment opportunity? A doctor with a gorgeous new office seems like the perfect person to ask about investing in blankyclip. It is quite a surprise after we've finished discussing yogurt, teething crackers, and puréed meats when Dr. Hiller tells me, "I didn't have the money to build this office. All this came from Bank of America!"

Bank of America? Wowsa. "May I ask for the name of your contact there?" I say.

One week later, and I have a meeting at Bank of America! Their stock is trading at nearly $46 a share, a high for them. They're riding the wave that's lifting the entire market to all-time highs. They must have tons of cash, and I'm going to ask them for some. I meet with Jeffrey and Shawn. Shawn is the guy who helped Dr. Hiller get her loan, and Jeffrey is the guy from the branch I'd be working with. I show them my prototype and talk about my invention and my business. They tell me that they love helping people start businesses and that they admire what I'm doing. Go, small business! Shawn says he usually works with doctors, but he'll see what he can do. It feels surprisingly easy to talk to them, and they seem to want to help me. Last I checked, I've not been able to get any investors to help me manufacture my product, so it seems like a loan is going to be the only route for me. The upside is that I'll keep my ownership of blankyclip. The downside is that I'll be borrowing money from a bank.

When I follow up with Jeffrey, he says he thinks he can get me a loan for $25,000. Nice, but it won't be enough for me to manufacture. I explain I'll need more than that, and he says he'll try. Feels like I'm turning a corner in the money-raising department.

Still August 2007. Over a year after our partnership dissolved, I meet with my Orthodox guys, and it's like no time has passed. I think the same junk food wrappers and soda cans litter their conference room. I tell them I have financing and am ready to manufacture. "Please get me quotes for an order of three different blankyclip designs totaling ten thousand pieces," I say with incredulous confidence. It occurs to me that I have made a person and delivered her since we last met, and these men do not know this about me.

It's going to cost more money than I have—and more money than the bank wants to loan me—to manufacture my blankyclips and market them and do everything I need to do. I call Jeffrey at Bank of America, but he doesn't have better news for me. The bank's still holding at the $25,000 limit. If I can get each blankyclip for $2 and the minimum order from the factories is 10,000 units, that's $20,000 just for the clips. I need to ship them here, store them, package them somehow, order blankets, and also keep the business running. Come on, Bank of America. The global economy is strong, and you're raking in the cash! Loan me some more of it!

SOLID AS A ROCK

August 2007. British bank Northern Rock's solid business plan—borrow money, use that money to extend mortgages, and then resell those mortgages in the international marketplace—ran into a bit of a snag when it couldn't find enough buyers for said mortgages. Suddenly, it couldn't afford to repay its loans. Individual depositors at Northern Rock panicked and lined up outside its seventy-five branches to withdraw all their savings, like now. Northern Rock hurried to the Bank of England for some extra cash. This kicked off two courses of action that would resonate for years to come: 1) Large-scale infusion of cash from national banks to save (or attempt to save) private ones. Like the $38 billion that the U.S. Fed pumped into the financial markets in August 2007. And the $130 billion that the European Central Bank did in, well, Europe. And the $27 billion that the Bank of England floated Northern Rock. 2) Subprime mortgage crisis panic. Financial markets around the world began plummeting because somebody figured out that lending lots and lots of money to people and institutions who couldn't afford to pay you back was something that even most first-year MBA students would recommend against.

In the middle of all this, I score a meeting with a huge player in the baby products industry. She's also head of marketing at the makeup company where my husband now works. Happily, this company is much closer to our home, so his long commute is over.

Paula is a twig—if twigs were made of hardened steel and fireworks. She's been one of my heroes for years. She started a baby product store that's become the standard of high-end baby retail. I've read about her while I've been developing blankyclip, and I can't believe I'm now meeting with her to show her the finished product.

She moves with utter confidence, like a force of nature. I have to wait in her office while she finishes three other conversations. While we talk, people come in to get her take on a particular color or a packaging sample. What she says carries a lot of weight. And she loves my blankyclips!

"I wish they were around when I had kids," she tells me. "I remember how my blanket would always fall off the stroller." I tell her

I'm waiting to hear about a bank loan, and she says, "You're very smart to get a loan. I had private investors help start my company, and because of that I lost control of the company."

I'm having one of those "I can't believe I'm sitting here" moments with someone who was able to walk into a meeting with private equity investors and walk away with $7 million to start a business. I've only raised $25,000 and am hoping that a bank will give me a big enough loan to move forward. Yet she's telling me how smart I am to keep creative control of my company.

We discuss how blankyclips and a blanket should be packaged. She sketches the front of a barn and wonders how it would look to attach the blankyclips to a piece of cardboard and wrap the cardboard around the blanket. A barn? I mean, maybe for my sheep blankyclip, but for the bear? The idea is so far from what I would want that I'm stunned. She seems to be pulling random thoughts together, and I watch the pedestal I've placed her on crumble. It's clear she's a busy woman, so I extricate myself graciously and thank her for her time and input. As I drive away, I feel like the lesson for me is that no one "out there" has all the answers. I have to trust my own vision.

And then—voilà!—Jeffrey from Bank of America calls. They've agreed to lend me $50,000 so I can begin the manufacturing process. They're going to open a liquid CD where the money will live, and I can transfer it over to my checking account as I need it. The move from $25,000 to $50,000 makes all the difference in the world. Now I can put in my first production order. I'm so relieved that I can now focus on things other than money raising.

I hurry to tell my Orthodox guys to find me a factory I can afford. The one that sent the great plush toy prototypes is way too expensive. They gave a quote of $5.25 per clip, which is out of the question. My guys have a contact in China who is looking for a factory that will give us a better price.

There is another reason to celebrate. On the day before she turns nine months old, my baby girl looks at me and says, "Mama." Heaven. Maybe one day she'll say, "Mama, I'm so amazed that you secured the initial capital to start blankyclip."

⁂

September 2007. The USPTO has granted my third Extension Request on my trademark. Another $150 has bought me six more months. I'm allowed five total Extension Requests, which means I'm down to two—eighteen more months in all—before I either have to start selling blankyclips or abandon my registered trademark. Tick-tock, people!

At Target, I do more research on baby blankets. I buy My Blankee, a beautiful plush blanket I've seen given at baby showers. The company's address is in Los Angeles. The packaging ribbon around My Blankee is so nice that I decide to call the company to find out who makes their ribbon. They're a successful business, so it's great that they're willing to help me out. I have no idea how else I would find a company that prints ribbon for packaging. Their ribbon guy is George. He's Persian and has an office in downtown LA. It's beyond fun to be discussing ribbon for the packaging of blankyclips!

I meet with a new accountant, Don, who comes recommended by a friend. He has a reputation for being very conservative and very knowledgeable about corporate accounting. He seems like exactly the kind of accountant I need. For starters, he doesn't meet clients in his pajamas. (Don't get me started on *that* guy.) He tells me, "You'll need to get your corporate papers in order, stock certificates, etc. I'm not thrilled with the agreements you created for friends who invested, but handshake deals with friends are permissible by law to a certain extent, and you'll probably be fine." He's kind of scaring me.

December 2007. I get my next quote from a factory in China, $3.35 per clip. That's still way too expensive, but we're moving in the right direction.

HOME ECONOMICS

Third quarter 2007. Merrill Lynch wrote down $8.4 billion in losses because of the housing crisis. Financial analysts with serious tones of voice seemed very, *very* concerned about this. $8.4 billion did feel like a lot of money, but most nonfinancial analysts with more playful tones of voice figured institutions like Merrill Lynch had plans to absorb that kind of loss.

January 2008. My Orthodox guys have found the only factory in China with pricing close to what I'm looking for, $2.20 a clip. That's $22,000 for a first order of 10,000, which is doable, but the samples they send us have a lot of problems. Not being able to speak each other's language makes it tricky to communicate what the problems are, so we're sending drawings since words have been failing us. Our interpreter, Peter, seems to understand what I'm having issues with, but maybe he doesn't, because the samples haven't been getting much better. We're talking about design issues that are difficult to put into words and even more difficult when you don't use the same words.

GOODNIGHT, MOON. GOODNIGHT, BED.
GOODNIGHT, FURNITURE STORE.

When her son was two, the blankyclip lady bought her son's bed from Wickes Furniture Store. Her eighteen installment payments didn't save Wickes from filing for Chapter 11 bankruptcy protection in February 2008. Within a month, every Wickes store—forty-three of them at one point during its thirty-seven-year history—closed for good.

Time to file Extension Request #4 for my trademark application. Hard to believe another six months have gone by. I'm down to my last extension. Twelve more months before I need to start selling or lose my trademark. Breathe, Adrienne, breathe.

TA-TA, TALBOTS

After twenty years in operation, with over sixty-six stores, Talbot Kids went out of business. So what? Businesses tended to go under, even in the healthiest of economies. Most economists didn't even blink at the Talbot Kids and Wickes Furniture news.

March 2008. I visit Toys "R" Us to look at bear faces. They have a huge stuffed animal section with an entire row of bear plush toys staring at me in disbelief that I think they can help me fix my bear problem. I snap pictures of the faces I think are the cutest. Our bear prototype is the one that needs the most work. It just doesn't look at all like a bear. It's missing the big snout area. Somehow the factory has not understood how to fix it, so I'm hoping that pictures will help. Are there no bears in China?

Maybe I'm more stressed out with juggling mommyhood and the business than I realize. Today I take my fifteen-month-old daughter to an outdoor kids' concert so she can be stimulated and enriched by the hip sounds of Melissa Green. We pop into the nearby Baby Gap where the sounds cease to be enriching. The wallet I need to pay for my nephew's birthday gift is gone. I made the mistake of thinking I could rest the wallet on top of my baby's stroller while flipping through the sale rack one last time. In that span of a minute or two, someone has grabbed it out of the sunshade. Dagny watches me get hysterical and cry. The driver's license and the credit cards and the library cards and the baby photos and all those little treasures we keep in our giant wallets have been taken from me. From on top of my baby's stroller while she is sitting inside the stroller? A store employee tells me, "It's been happening a lot lately."

"People crying?"

"No, stealing."

Dagny stares at me wide-eyed as Mama has gone from singing songs about the alphabet to singing the blues. I think it's the first time she's seen me cry like this. I'm surprised at how much cry is pouring out of me. The other customers don't seem to mind me, focused as they are on hunting for the good sale items. We finally leave after a sweep of the store does not end with the discovery of my wallet or the thief. I don't have my parking lot ticket (already validated!) because of course it's in my wallet. I'm all out of cry at this point, but a phone call to the store manager helps the attendant understand why I need to be allowed out of the parking structure without a ticket. An exception is made, and he lifts the exit bar for me grudgingly. This public moment of despair is the first one that my infant daughter is witness to, and that feels significant.

I meet with George about getting ribbon with my logo printed on it. The more inexpensive ribbon feels chintzy, and I'm willing to pay a little bit more and get a noticeably better product. I like that I can actually go and meet with George because his business is here in LA. He's very sweet, and he reminds me of my grandfather. He keeps telling me that I shouldn't worry because he's going to take good care of me and get me a good price. He came to this country with $5, left everything behind except his family, and now has a prosperous business. Go, small business! I love working with people like George who engage so personally. The ribbon I choose is white and satiny, perfect for a high-end retailer like Babystyle. I can't wait to see my logo printed on my beautiful ribbon!

The gravity of the financial industry's situation still eludes me because I'm too busy jumping for joy from a call I get from Frank at Bank of America. I don't know Frank, but I love him. He asks me if I want to increase my line of credit from $50,000 to $100,000—a hundred friggin' thousand! He has a new program that Bank of America is offering, and I eagerly accept. We handle it all by phone and fax. I don't even have to meet with him. This is incredible! Now I can start production and get my ribbon made and put up a website and go to trade shows and really get this company moving.

BLANK (CHECK) OF AMERICA
As the calendar flipped to 2008, Bank of America flipped out at all the bargains available on the failing-financial-institution discount rack. For heaven's sake, Countrywide Mortgage (which had just months ago received an emergency $11 billion loan) had a big ol' Will Take Any Offer sticker pasted to its general ledger. But BofA wanted to make its own financials look as robust as possible in these trying times, so what's a lending institution to do when it wants more assets to add to its balance sheet? Well, the smarties over there figured out that loans are considered assets, so they added a bunch of those to give themselves more black than red.

The technician who runs the enormous ribbon-printing machine is covered in ink. The machine is so massive that he needs a ladder to add black ink to make the purple in my logo a darker hue. The ribbon runs through the various stages of ink application, all incredible to watch. The logo looks gorgeous printed on the white satiny ribbon.

Then George takes me to meet a guy who can make my hang tags. He's in the neighborhood, but we need to drive, so I hop into George's Camry. The guy shows me different standard sizes and different stocks of paper. The corners will be rounded. My designer Patty loves rounded corners. This tag will be attached to the ribbon and feature photos as well as information about the product. I can't believe how much I enjoy talking to a guy who makes hang tags.

Now I need a professional product photographer, a whole different animal from taking photos of people. Going through websites of photographers who do this, I see how they can make a plate or a shoe look either amazing or totally uninteresting. Cost is always an issue for me, so I need to find someone both great and affordable.

I'm back on the late-night calls to China. One of the Orthodox guys and I first get on the phone, and then he conferences in China. We call Peter, the translator, who's dealing with the factory, where no one speaks a word of English. I'm shocked at the way my Orthodox guy speaks to Peter. He orders him around angrily, all for a product I invented. I want our talks to be more civil, but my Orthodox guy tells me, "This is the way you get things done over there." It's almost midnight in LA. I'm in my pajamas in my home office, yet I'm so uncomfortable with this call.

A few days later I make brownies for some of my initial investors. They want to discuss their investment in blankyclip, and I need to fill them in on the change that we're now going to be manufacturing instead of getting into a licensing deal. I'm worried about their possible disappointment that they won't have a revenue stream quite yet, and they are in fact disappointed, but they also love my brownies. I am sincerely grateful that they invested in my idea, and I do not take this responsibility lightly.

<hr />

April 2008. Ruth has issued my utility patent. Oh happy day! I am the proud owner of US Patent No. 7,356,889. I love that number so much. It's crazy that we filed for this patent in June of 2005, and even crazier that I had the idea for this product when Eli was two months old. He's now four and a half, and I'm now an official mom inventor.

5

A Hole in the Floor

Still April 2008. My stomach is doing somersaults. Will someone please remind me why I decided to invent a product and then manufacture it? On top of the product samples and the blanket sourcing and the trademarks and the QuickBooks and the packaging design and the etc., there's the giant trade show in September to figure out.

Henry the patent attorney isn't satisfied that I've been awarded my utility patent. He thinks I can be better protected, so he recommends I file for a continuation application, which requests protection for claims not recognized under my first patent. This costs me another $1,500, but if I end up with stronger protection of my idea, then it is well worth it.

Gary and I create a timeline. The trade show is less than five months away, and I don't have my product yet. We figure out by what day blankyclips need to be finished in order to leave enough time for them to arrive from China. The date we come up with is way too close to today.

It's troubling that the factory keeps sending me blankyclip samples that are not acceptable, and now they want to start charging me for them. They don't seem to understand that if only they would make the changes I keep asking them to make, I wouldn't need so many samples. How is this factory suddenly going to make the product I want in the time I need them to?

May 2008. I meet with a product photographer and bring my shot list so we can discuss everything I want out of this photo shoot. The list is long, as I'll need photos for my website as well as my hang tag and my brochure. Plus, there are three designs of blankyclips, so I'll need three versions of everything. I don't think he's the right photographer for me. I'm just not getting much oomph from him.

BEAR MARKET

Bear Stearns disappeared. The financial services firm, which went from $172 a share in January 2007 to $5.33 just over a year later, was sold to JPMorgan Chase for $1.2 billion. $1.2 billion? That's a lot of money, the uninformed exclaimed. But they were set straight when reminded that at the end of 2006 Bear Stearns was valued at $66.7 billion. In fact, in one month—February 2008 to March 2008—Bear Stearns stock dropped from $93 a share to that lowly $5.33. One month! JPMorgan Chase originally agreed to buy Bear Stearns for $2 a share before feeling sorry for their three-piece-suited brethren and upping the price to $10.

It occurs to me that I need to know what info Li & Fung will put on the blanket tag, so I ask them. Then I find out that it is not a tag but a "care label," and by the way, what's my RN? Which is how I find out that I need a registered number from the Federal Trade Commission and that all imported textiles must have an RN on the care label. The FTC issues these numbers to U.S. businesses that manufacture, import, distribute, or sell products covered by the Textile, Wool, and Fur Acts—as in plush toys and blankets.

It's a wonder I can sleep at night.

I meet with the Orthodox guys about the latest batch of blankyclip samples. The placement of the animals' heads is still not right. The bear's face is still very strange and not bear-like. The different designs don't work as a unit. The bellies need to be the same size, and the arms need to be consistent. It's all so difficult to manage from so far away.

The good news is that I have found a photographer. After researching, networking, and doing lots of digging, I meet with a guy whose photos are amazing. He gets product photography, and he gets what I need to accomplish. He's willing to lower his rate a bit for me, so the search is over. Now we just need to set up the shoot.

June 2008. I take a trip to Home Depot in search of shelves to put in the garage for all the blankyclip elements: ribbons, hang tags, order forms, envelopes, stationery, and on and on. I'm in need of some serious organizing. All I wanted was a safe, cute, and effective way to secure my baby's blanket to his stroller, and now I'm turning my garage into a warehouse.

IT'S MORE THAN THE CHEESE THAT'S FULL OF HOLES

In May 2008, UBS, the largest Swiss banking institution in the world, announced 5,500 layoffs. The losses they incurred from mortgage-backed securities were too great to ignore. More and more, the financial industry began showing the impact of the subprime mortgage crisis.

All this bad news about the financial industry is coming thick and fast, but I barely register it. These huge firms and their billion-dollar losses surely won't have any impact on a mom inventor and her needs, which are in the mere thousands of dollars. The bad news feels very far away as I begin to think seriously about the trade show. I'll need furniture pieces or marketing displays that I can ship easily and that will nicely show off my product.

More bad samples arrive from China. This is my first production run, and it has to look great, and right now the samples look far from great, which is why I'm packing a suitcase and arranging for baby-sitting. I'm going to be traveling to China, by myself, to visit the factory and get the necessary changes made.

I arrange a meeting with the folks at Li & Fung, my blanket source, for when I'm in Hong Kong. They email me about the flammability test, which is necessary for baby blankets. There's some concern that the stock blankets haven't been treated for flammability. Suddenly I'm thinking that I should be treated for flammability because my blood is about to boil with this news. The blankets can only be treated when they're being made, so it is a huge relief to learn that they have indeed been treated. Must there be so many moments of panic over undisclosed information that seems so critical?

My request to meet seems to have accelerated things. Li & Fung asks to get in touch with my shipping company, Expeditors, to arrange for the shipment of my blankets. I'm not just a mom inventor, I'm about to become a mom importer too.

❧————❧

Still June 2008. While I thought I'd be traveling alone to China, my "friend" arrives just in time to leave with me for LAX. Were they being ironic or idiotic when they gave that little nickname to a woman's monthly cycle? I pack the absorbent accoutrements I'll need for my friend and wait for my cab to the airport.

The cab arrives a few minutes late, and then the cabbie can't figure out how to run my credit card through his little machine, so he insists I pay cash. I refuse because I don't have much cash with me, and I need this expense on my credit card statement. He's surly, almost menacing, so I grab my bags and get out of the cab. All this takes about half an hour, and now I'm panicked that I'm going to miss my flight. Gary comes to the rescue; he manages to find a babysitter and drives me to LAX just in time.

I hurry through the concourses and get to my gate for the eighteen-hour flight. I decide to spring for business class tickets because the people I know who have made this trip over and over again, like Gary and my Orthodox guys, have advised me that if I fly business class on the red-eye, I'll arrive ready to deal with what lies ahead of me.

Sitting in business class definitely gives me the feeling that I own a business. I'll take a piece of confidence from wherever I can get it at this point. The menu helps matters, as does the glass of sauvignon blanc. I'm flying China Airlines, and I already feel like I'm in a different world. While my fellow passengers seem to carry the heaviness of "Let me get settled in for this interminable journey across the Pacific," I'm so looking forward to the interminable journey across the Pacific. I'm going to be alone for how long? With nothing to do but read or watch a movie or sleep? Nowhere I have to be but here. No kids and no computer. It's like a suspension of time. As we roll down the runway and go wheels up, the stress flows away from me, and for the first time in a very long time, I rest.

When I change planes in Taiwan, my calm evaporates. I have to figure out where to go, and the signs still are not in English. People push by me to catch flights, and I have to go through another security line and have my carry-on bags screened once again. I follow the mass of humanity and hope I'm heading in the right direction. I pass stores that sell foods I don't recognize in bins. I'm the odd man out, as most everyone is Asian and has the right currency. It's all very unsettling, and I can't wait for my next flight so I can get some water.

I'm not sure what day it is (my body still thinks it's in Los Angeles) as I get off the plane in Hong Kong. I look for Peter, the translator, near the Burger King in the airport. We find each other, which is good since my Blackberry doesn't seem to be set up for international calls, or else I'm not using the right code. I've been traveling for days, it seems, and Peter asks me if I'm hungry. I'm not, as I've done nothing but sit on an airplane and eat. But he is, so we go into the Burger King and he orders a hamburger. I'm in my business suit, and my period's hit me full force, and I feel like I could use a shower. But I'm in Hong Kong, and it's the start of a business day, and we're about to head to Shenzhen in mainland China, which is a three-hour trek. Peter finishes his hamburger, and we begin our journey to Shenzhen. We take a van service that leaves from the airport. Five minutes into the drive I'm sound asleep. I wake up when I hear the van door open. Wow, that was fast! But we're not anywhere near Shenzhen yet. We're at a security checkpoint, about to enter China. We have to give our passports up for inspection. This is when it hits me that I am entering a Communist country. I'm nervous as the guard looks over my passport. I'm in a van heading into a country that is known to treat its people in a severe way, and what on earth could I do about it if they took me away right now? I'm grateful when the van door closes and we're on our way.

After more than three hours, which I have mostly slept through, the van lets us off at a Shenzhen train station. The factory owner is there to drive us to his factory. He doesn't speak a word of English, so we nod and smile to each other— something I will do a lot of over the next few days. I'm acutely aware of being the American who's having a product made in a country where the labor is cheap. I imagine the factory owner and Peter think I'm a millionaire or something. We're all holding on to whatever stereotypical image we have of each other to make sense of this awkward situation.

We get into the factory owner's beat-up Mao-era Jeep. I'm in the backseat. Behind me in the storage area there are rolls of foam and fabric and odd manufacturing kinds of things. We head to the factory as the odd nut or bolt rolls around behind me and the sound of Mandarin wafts from the front seat.

It's a surprise when we stop, and I'm told we're having lunch. The place we've come to is like something out of a movie. It's a wooden hotel or motel or restaurant—I can't quite tell. There are steps up to the entrance, and they are lined with Chinese women in uniforms all smiling at me. They're wearing little white *Sound of Music* hats and dresses with white aprons. As we enter, we pass tanks of fish. There are more waitstaff inside, smiling at me as I walk by. We're taken into a private dining room. I'm asked if I'd like to come choose my lunch from the fish tanks. First, I find my way to the bathroom, which I am so happy to see. Gary warned me to not drink much for a few hours before landing in Hong Kong, as he knew the drive to Shenzhen would present a challenge for a woman who needs to pee every half hour. There are no places to stop along the way. So I hurry to the restroom, and when I return I'm by the fish tanks, filled with all kinds of spiny and gooey creatures. I'm not going to say I eat shrimp because I can see the shrimp walking around with their huge antennae and legs—we're a long way from the frozen ones in the bag—so I say I like vegetables and rice and they look at me like I'm crazy.

Back at our table, the factory owner sits eating some kind of appetizer while he watches the black-and-white television provided in the private rooms. He and I can't talk to each other anyway, but it's beyond strange to be having my first business lunch in China this way. Peter struggles between trying to make small talk with me and with the factory owner, his eyes straying to the compelling soap opera on the TV. It's dramatic stuff, as far as I can make out.

Main courses begin to arrive. The factory owner devours his shrimp and rips off the heads, and I can't tell where the legs are ending up. "My stomach isn't feeling too well," I say, which isn't entirely a lie. Fuzzy things arrive in small bowls, and I'm getting how misleading the whole Chinese restaurant concept in America really is. I don't see a chow fun in my future anytime soon.

Finally, we get to the factory, and I meet the factory owner's wife. She's responsible for the sewing and design work, which basically means she made all the samples I have received, which means she didn't make all the changes I asked for. I'm eager to get into a discussion about how to fix the prototypes, but first I convey that I need a restroom. She grabs a roll of toilet paper that's almost finished and indicates I should follow her. We head down the staircase and out the door. Then we traipse across the dirt road over to an open store/hut where an old woman and big pots of food sit on the ground among lots of odds and ends. I can't make out if she sells the food or not, but anyway I'm told to use the bathroom there. It's a small dirty room with only enough space for a toilet that holds the tiniest bit of water. I manage, but is there really no bathroom in the factory?

I find my way back across the dirt road and up the stairs. The entire factory is made up of the office space where the husband and wife work and an open area where about seventy-five employees sew at their workstations. There are bits of fabric and foam stuffing and thread strewn about. The workers look young, but not too young. I was worried about this, with what you hear goes on in China, but they actually look like they're in their late teens and early twenties.

Via Peter, I tell the wife what doesn't work for me about the samples. She says she'll make a new sample for me and it will be ready in a few hours. I guess this is why I flew to China.

The husband decides that we should go look for fabric and foam, so we pile back into his Jeep. We arrive at a fabric market, or rather a fabric stall. It's very small, and the fabrics are hanging everywhere. I feel half a world away (literally) from Michael Levine, the retail mega fabric store in downtown Los Angeles. The factory owner already has the white fabric for the sheep and the yellow for the duck, but he needs me to pick out a brown bear fabric since he's not found an exact match for my sample made at the expensive factory. I pick one, and everyone agrees it is a good choice. Then we head to the foam guy.

The foam store is a version of the fabric stall, but it has a front door. There are so many different kinds of foam options all rolled up. The place stinks of chemicals and is amazingly dirty. I squish foam samples between my fingers, trying to imagine which one has the right degree of thickness to cover my plastic clip and keep the fingers of the babies of America safe. I'm amazed that I am making all these decisions. Somehow, I thought "the factory" would know what to do and "the factory" would make the product the way I wanted it, and what ends up being "the factory" is a husband and wife and some young (but not too young) Chinese people sitting at long tables with sewing machines on them, in a rundown building on a dirt road on the outskirts of Shenzhen.

Next stop is the tooling factory, where they've made the mold for the inner clip of a blankyclip, a plastic-injected mold of the two pieces that form the clip. It's a bare-bones space with lots of different metal molds on large stands, and it smells of grease and chemicals. The men are wearing loose pants and sleeveless undershirts that we used to call wife beaters. I don't see goggles or protective jackets or anything that resembles suitable covering for working in such an extreme environment. They're making metal molds and then filling them with hot liquid plastic, and no part of their wispy bodies is protected. I'm presented with my mold, which is about the size of a toaster oven. I'm shown the engraving that states the name of my company and my patent number, which will end up on every clip they manufacture. The two pieces of the clip are held together with an inner coil, and a huge bag of these coils (10,000 of them) sits in the factory owner's office, wound with the exact amount of tension that makes a blankyclip safe for babies.

Last stop on the manufacturing tour is the embroidery factory where the noses and eyes and mouths are sewn onto the fabric. There is a row of sewing machines synchronized so that you can have twenty or so machines running at the same time. The pattern is computerized, and then the machines do their thing, creating noses or eyes or mouths for the plush part of a toy.

It's absolutely crazy seeing all the elements and how each one is produced in its own little factory. The fabric people, the foam people, the mold people, the coil people. Then the outer plush is put together at "my" factory, where the final assembly of the elements comes together. The factory owner's wife is responsible for creating the pattern for the outer plush, the animal design that covers the clip. Then her pattern is used to make a metal mold that will stamp out the desired shape of the plush fabric. On a massive slab of metal, a sandwich-shaped cutter called a die cut stamps the fabric. The metal die cut was made prior to my arrival, and now I watch it in action. This one piece of metal will be used to cut all the plush fabrics, which will cover the inner clips.

I am such a long way from Tim's garage with Eli playing in the yard that it's ridiculous!

The factory owner sits down with the workers to discuss how to wrap the newly purchased foam around the plastic clip. He wants to use the smallest amount of foam to cover the clip entirely, with a little extra padding for the area where the clip ends meet. As I watch him figure this all out, I feel incredibly out of place in my Ann Taylor Loft suit and my Aerosoles sensible heels. I can contribute nothing to this process. Not surprising that I can sense how much he isn't crazy about my being there, the silent observer and scrutinizer.

I'm beyond tired. I've made sure to take a pass on all the offerings of tea in the factory owner's office, as I have been warned back home of the danger of drinking water at a factory. They drink tea from these thimble-sized cups, and there are tea leaves all over the small tea tray. I'd forgotten what it was like to be sitting next to a smoker. I don't have to experience this often in Los Angeles, but here in Shenzhen the office is a cloud of smoke that I'm unable to escape.

The factory owner comes up with a system he likes for securing the foam to the clips. And while he is trying to use as little foam as possible to keep his costs down, I'm there asking him to use as much foam as possible, especially on the area where the clip ends meet. I want this area extra padded. He isn't thrilled because we have already agreed on a price, and the more foam he uses the less profit he makes, but he comes up with a way to double the foam.

Now it's time to place the animal plush cover over the entire clip. I am beholding the creation of a blankyclip! But then I watch as it tips over, and suddenly the joy is gone.

The factory owner's wife glares at me as I explain that the animal blankyclips need to be able to sit up on their own if they're displayed on a table or shelf. They can do so much more than be clipped to a stroller if they can sit up. It's a little thing, but it will make a huge difference down the line. There's too much fabric on the base of the clips. I'm really upset. The factory owner has seen my prototypes from the more expensive factory ($5 a clip), which don't tip over, so he knows his shouldn't either. Still, he gives me an argument via Peter. "The pattern has already been made, and from this pattern the die cut has been made, and this is how the other ten thousand pieces will come out. The die cut has been cast, and it's too late to change it." I'm sure the factory owner adds a few expletives in Mandarin, but Peter doesn't translate that part.

My eyes go wide. More words I don't understand are exchanged, and what happens next is absolutely unbelievable. A shirtless man arrives and takes away the die cut. We wait in the office. For about an hour. I can't even calculate how many hours I've been up at this point. Twenty-four? Thirty-six? If I left LA at 10:00 p.m., now it's . . . I have no idea. I'm thirsty, but I have to manage my fluid intake, although I'm now allowed to use the factory bathroom (I knew there had to be one). It's a tiled room with a hole in the floor, a handle on the wall to hold on to while squatting, and a red bucket of water with a cup floating on top. I assume these last items are meant for rinsing the area around the hole (the one in the floor). I'm having my period and squatting over a hole in the frickin' floor in my nice suit, and the best I can do is try not to drink too much of my bottled water even though I'm feeling so dehydrated from the flight and the smoke and the day that started eons ago when my taxi was late.

Like a magic trick, the shirtless man reappears with a newly sized die cut. Somehow, in the span of an hour, the metal mold that cuts out the pattern of the fabric covering my blankyclips has been shortened by about an inch. I'm floored. This is something that would probably take six weeks in the States. The technology available on this dirt road is staggering. Did I mention that the man was not wearing a shirt?

We take the die cut out into the alley to a big table with a large metal cutting apparatus. The factory owner puts the die cut onto it and cuts out a piece of brown bear fabric with a loud whack. I am standing at the place where the fabric was going to be cut into a piece an inch or so too big. Because I flew to China and saw that there was too much fabric, the fix was made. It's hard not having someone to tell all this to as I'm experiencing it.

The factory owner's wife sews the piece into the bear shape, and then the moment of truth. She slips it over the foam-covered clip, and voilà! My blankyclip can sit up without tipping over. I'm relieved and joyous. This is why I flew to China. How on earth could we have worked all this out across the planet from each other?

After some Mandarin chitchat, Peter suggests that this is a good place to stop for the day. I couldn't agree more. The factory owner drives Peter and me to the train station where he picked us up. Do I want to stop for some dinner first? Ha! No, thank you. Peter doesn't need to go to Hong Kong, so he points me in the right direction for my train and hustles off. Suddenly, I'm at the ticket counter needing to buy a train ticket to Hong Kong. The ticket seller doesn't speak

English, but she understands me when I say Hong Kong. There are hundreds of people shuffling past me in a rush to catch their trains, and I'm baffled as to which way to go in this giant Chinese version of Grand Central Station. There is truly not an English-speaking person anywhere and not a single sign that I can read. A Chinese woman takes pity on me. "Hong Kong?" she asks, and I nod yes, and she shows me where I need to go. My angel.

The train is packed, so I have to stand. In my sensible heels, but heels, nonetheless. With my briefcase and luggage. I stick out like a sore American thumb. My feet hurt. I'm starving. I'm dehydrated. I'm having cramps. I stand like this for about two hours before a seat opens up just minutes before we arrive in Hong Kong.

I get off the train. Gary has explained that the underground tunnel I'm in has an exit that will lead me close to my hotel. I'm relieved to see signs in both English and Cantonese. I've been in this subway station before, when I splurged on some earrings, but I didn't really take it in. There are expensive shops everywhere, although they're all closed. Clinique makeup. Benetton. Designer everything. All so brightly lit and clean. Who knew there could be such fancy shopping in a subway station?

I'm overjoyed to find the entrance to the Renaissance Hotel. After I check in, I immediately order room service. Something recognizable. Pasta. I take a shower. Dinner arrives. I take one bite and pass out, my face inches from my plate.

The next morning, I have a meeting with Vincent and Nicole at Li & Fung. My blanket order is already underway, but it's nice to meet them and establish more of a relationship.

Vincent says, "We can get anything you want made."

Nicole chimes in. "Just let us know what you want, and we'll find a factory that can do it."

Their English is perfect, and the Li & Fung offices are super snazzy. They've got displays of many of the products they manufacture or source, and there are a lot of them. The lighting is white-blue cool, and the floors are polished, slick and gorgeous. I'm in another world here in Hong Kong from the one in Shenzhen—just an unbearable train ride away.

⁂

I arrive and learn that the factory owner's wife stayed and worked on the prototypes until late in the night, and three new designs are finished. The bear's face now looks like a bear's face, the duck's hands now go in the right direction, and the sheep looks cuter than ever. We can't speak a word to each other, but she can see how pleased I am. I had to come to China to do this. Hard to believe what got accomplished in twenty-four hours. I visited the factory that's going to make my blankyclips. I helped design and create the product I'm now going to sell. I peed in a hole in the floor. Mind-blowing.

I'm delighted to be back on the long train ride to Hong Kong, my work in Shenzhen done. There was so much discomfort dealing with the smoky office area, the incredible thirst, the language barrier, and the overall uneasiness of being in a factory where the workers are hunched over sewing machines and I'm the demanding American businesswoman. I decide to celebrate my victorious journey by treating myself to dinner at Nobu in the InterContinental Hotel. Oh, the shame of it, but seeing the Hong Kong harbor lights and the ferries going by while I'm reading a book and dining on the most amazing sushi ever really does not suck.

In the morning, I meet with Intertek to discuss the safety testing my product needs before it can be sold in the U.S. They are the experts of safety testing, and I find out what the tests are and how much they cost. Intertek will take my product and bang it around and do God knows what to it to see if it holds up. My main concern is that I pass

CLIPPED

the ASTM F963 test "for birth and up." I'll need to put a tag on the blankyclips, and that tag has to say that they've passed this test, which means they are safe for babies in the U.S., which in turn means I can sell them in the States. The Orthodox guys haven't told me I need this test. They haven't really been organizing much for me, and I wonder what would happen with my product if I didn't take it upon myself to find these things out.

My time in China is almost over. I can't wait to get back to my family. Peter has decided to meet me at the airport before my flight for a wrap-up. He feels good about the progress we made at the factory. "It's very hard to understand the kind of design changes you wanted by talking about it on the phone," he says. "The factory is happy to have this job, but mainly because they are looking forward to the giant order you will place when you begin selling in Walmart. At this point they are losing money on such a small ten-thousand-piece order." He laughs a little to lighten his bummer message.

"Oh, yes," I tell him. "I'm looking forward to selling blankyclips at Walmart too!" I let out a little chuckle.

"We want an order for millions of blankyclips!" he says. And now his laugh is even more committed.

We are both laughing, but the two of us have no idea how funny this conversation truly is.

6

Hysterical Woman

Goodness, still June 2008. The photo shoot for my marketing materials is coming up, and I need a few props. I go to Ikea and grab a bunch of wicker baskets. They've got a little sheepskin rug that might be cute to put the blankyclips on. Or I can use it to take a nap while I pretend there isn't a trade show to prepare for.

Branding is one of those buzzwords that's lost a lot of its force through ubiquitous overuse. But in spite of its painful origins (Really? A red-hot piece of shaped iron pressed onto an animal's flesh?), if I get it right, branding will help my potential customers leapfrog over questions like "Is it a high-quality product?" and "How cool will I be if I use it?" straight to "It fits my lifestyle, and I must have it!" So, what is the blankyclip brand? Soft, cuddly, safe . . . what else?

The blankyclip hang tag will have a specific design, image, and feel that will communicate the blankyclip brand. The little plastic fasteners that connect tags to clothes and stuffed animals get attached by a hang tag gun. I'm at Michael Levine downtown to pick one up. I am sure as I purchase my hang tag gun and box of 10,000 fasteners it looks like I know what I'm doing, and I have a hang tag in need of attaching. I do not.

I'm back at Babies "R" Us to shop for the photo shoot. I need a nice-looking diaper bag (mine are trashed because I use them as diaper bags and not props) with no logos on it. I find a nondescript brown one that will work well. I pick up some fresh bibs and diaper cloths. I figure I can return whatever I don't use, so I get them in a range of colors. While I'm at it, I pick up a nice bouncy seat and a travel swing. I want to show all the uses for blankyclips and all the places they can attach to. I need a car seat too, but I can use my kids' old one since we'll be covering it with a blanket. The new Peg Perego stroller will be an important part of my trade show exhibit—no way I can use my old stroller after two babies. It feels crazy to be buying all this baby gear that's not for a baby, but it's a business expense and it's for pictures and a trade show, so it has to look gorgeous. It's fun to see what new gear is out there since I'm always checking to see if there's anything close to competition for a blankyclip. The answer, happily, is no.

I head to Brand Park in Glendale to pay for a permit and reserve the Japanese tea garden for the shoot. Now I'm official. I have a factory in China making goods for me, and I have a trade show to prep for. No more hiding in bushes to take pictures. It's a really pretty spot with lots of green everywhere, big trees and a little pond, and no one else will be allowed in because we have the permit to use it all day, until closing at 5:00 p.m.

All I need now is babies. I'll use my daughter, of course, but she's nineteen months old, so I'll need a younger baby as well. A French mom friend brings over her little baby girl so I can see if she's the right baby to use, and she's absolutely gorgeous. I'm so lucky that my friend is willing to let me photograph her baby and use her image for my marketing materials. She's a French baby and has the most beautiful perfect little French face ever. The mom is easygoing and totally wants to help me out in exchange for nothing. Maybe it's a thrill for her to have her baby's image preserved? I can't believe how easy it was to solve the I-need-a-baby problem.

I head over to the Juvenile Shop to look for cute clothes for my baby models. I have to think about this. The clothes can't pull focus from the product. They need to be subtle but attractive, neutral, not distracting, with no images, and they are not easy to find. I end up with a cute yellow outfit for Dagny at Naartjie in the mall, and a few options for the baby at Babies "R" Us. Since I'll be leaving bright and early for the shoot, I load up the car in the evening with all the gear, props, and of course blankyclips! I'm reminded of my days on the set as an actress. Now I'm the one with the shot list.

I'm getting ready for bed when the phone rings. It's my French mom friend. A virus has hit the family, and everyone is throwing up, including the baby. She's so sorry that she won't be able to be at the shoot in the morning. She must hear the panic in my voice, because she gives me the number of a Swedish mom who is her good friend and who might be available. She is! I tell her she's saving me big-time and thank her profusely. She says she can be there in the morning but not for long as she has a plane to catch later in the day. She's heading to Europe for the summer but will squeeze this in before she leaves. I'm so grateful to her for this generous act. Going to a park for a photo shoot before a flight to Europe? With a newborn? That's impressive.

The photographer has brought a lighting guy and a designer. I have a huge shot list, so we get right to it. We start with the Swedish three-month-old understudy who's playing "the sleeping baby who is kept nice and protected and whose blanket does not fall off or flap around and wake her." It's a happy miracle that she is actually asleep and does not wake up as we place her in the bouncy seat, cover her with a blanket, and clip the blanket with two bear blankyclips. She's gorgeous too, and looks perfectly at peace as she sleeps on and we get the shots we need. It's almost too much to see my idea in action, working as I had imagined, as we take pictures for my packaging.

On to what is probably the most important shot of the day: a stroller that has a blanket secured by blankyclips attached to the stroller shade on top and the food tray below, presumably covering a baby sleeping inside. I have my three different blankets—blue, pink, and ecru—but I pick the ecru one because it's gender-neutral. I can't have people thinking that blankyclips are meant only for girls or only for boys. They're for babies. The ecru blankets come with the yellow duck blankyclips, the background is green and lush, and the shot looks great in the monitor. A world of difference from any photo I ever took with my crappy little camera. My shot list also calls for pictures of the different blankyclips on different parts of the stroller, the sheep holding a bib on the side of the stroller, the bear clipping the unused blanket to the top of the stroller shade, and about a zillion more combinations.

We get fabulous shots, and then Dagny arrives with our babysitter, looking adorable in her new yellow outfit. She's playing "the toddler who wants to play with the clips, so thank goodness they're safe." She's curious about what Mommy is up to and proceeds with caution around all these new faces and the camera equipment. The designer sets out the pink blanket for her to sit on. Dagny's not so sure. I manage to coax her onto the blanket, and then I give her the white sheep blankyclip, primped and camera-ready, every piece of fluff in the right place. She throws the clip onto the grass with a big "No!" Excuse me? She's the toddler who has to show how much she loves blankyclips, and she's refusing? My own daughter?

The designer quickly scoops up the sheep clip and begins to pluck out the grass and dirt that are now all over it. I do my best to get Dagny to hold the blankyclip, look happy about it, and give us the shot we need. I had not counted on a toddler moment. Somehow, she understands that I need her to do something, so she's enjoying being defiant. Thankfully, she's nineteen months old and easily fooled, so when I start jumping up and down and making silly noises, she's distracted and humored and happens to be holding the sheep blankyclip, so take the picture *now*, Mr. Photographer! We get what we need. The shot ends up being perfect, and I am so pleased. There's an old show business adage, usually attributed to W. C. Fields, that goes, "Never work with children or animals." Somehow, I now have amazing shots of both my baby models and all my cooperative stuffed animals.

We get pictures of the sets of blankyclips as they'll be sold with the blankets, and we get pictures of each individual blankyclip clipped to every spot you might want to clip one. But it's suddenly 5:00 p.m. Our permit has expired while we're on the last few shots. They're closing the gates, people. The light is changing. I'm desperate to get it all.

"Your shot list was very optimistic," I'm informed by my photographer. And with one last shot of a blankyclip clipping a burp cloth onto the stroller, we're done.

The beauty of the digital age is that there's no waiting to develop pictures. At the end of the packing-up madness my photographer hands me a disc of JPGs and that's that.

At home, the freakout begins.

What was I thinking, only taking a picture of the stroller covered with the ecru blanket secured at top and bottom by the duck blankyclips? My most important shot of the day, showing the whole point of the product, but the problem with the ecru and the ducks is that beige and yellow are not strong colors and with all the sunlight you can't tell exactly what you're looking at. I thought I had to choose the one version that would appeal to both sexes, but now I've got something that doesn't pop and makes my product hard to see. What a stupid move on my part. I am so bummed.

But there's nothing to do about it now. I have lots more to worry about, and I do have some great shots. I love the one of Dagny holding the sheep clip. Miss No! For hours I sit looking through all the photos to see which ones speak best to the blankyclip brand. I have to pick the right ones for my hang tag and my brochure and the website.

A friend of mine who works at Disney is very familiar with trade shows and offers to help me design my booth. We meet for lunch, and she begins by drawing a booth to scale and sketching in furniture. That funny feeling in my stomach is starting up again as I'm overwhelmed by all the unknowns here. Where do I get the right furniture for the booth? Where do I get the signs and the posters? How do I make it look professional? She works with a Disney budget, and when I ask her how much these different display pieces she's suggesting might cost, she frankly has no idea. But she does know that I should put the important display pieces further into the booth so that people are guided up into the booth, where they'll stop and look at my product. Oh, and I should have brochures to hand out. And possibly some candy that has the company name or logo on it. Oh my goodness! So many decisions to make. And it all sounds so expensive.

I think she sees the fear in my eyes, because she offers, "Let's go wander through Ikea, and I'll point out what furniture pieces might work." I'm happy to have her help. The trade show in Las Vegas is coming up in less than three months. We look for little tables or stands that might work for blankyclip displays. Nothing seems right. I'll have to ship these items, so weight is a concern. She hasn't had to worry about any of this as Disney takes care of it all, so she really doesn't know how to help me do it on the cheap. The more we walk around the store, the more I can feel her slipping away from me. She wishes me all the best, but she has a job to get back to, and thanks so much for lunch!

It's a Sunday morning, and we're having brunch with the kids at a restaurant. This is a rare event, and it's as if the spirits have guided us here to Alcove Café, because as we are dining on overpriced eggs, in walks Matt Damon and his pregnant wife. This is an order-at-the counter joint, so like any reasonable woman in my position, I scoop up Dagny from her high chair and race to stand in line next to Matt and his wife. "She's gorgeous!" he says when he sees Dagny, and there we are, waiting for our turn to order, having a conversation about babies. I'm in heaven. With so much that makes me feel out of control, I am affirmed in some way by this little moment. If I can be bold enough to insert myself next to one of my favorite hunkster actors ("It's not your fault!"), maybe I can figure out how to create a booth for a trade show.

July 2008. I'm at the Juvenile Shop to speak with their buyer. I want to know what she thinks about the blankyclip gift set—a baby blanket and two blankyclips—and what she thinks it should retail for. I have to meet my costs and make a profit, but I want to make sure I price blankyclip at a number that makes sense, especially from the perspective of a sales channel where I can see my product actually selling. The buyer tells me that a retail price of $48 would be right on target. I'm feeling good that at least one store is on board to carry blankyclips. Of course, she hasn't exactly said so, but she isn't the warm and fuzzy type.

I catch a doom-and-gloom blurb just as I'm changing radio stations in my car, but I don't really hear it. I find Katy Perry singing, "I kissed a girl and I liked it, the taste of her cherry ChapStick." Katy reassures me, "It felt so wrong, it felt so right . . ."

WHAT THE BLANKYCLIP LADY DIDN'T HEAR

From July 2007 to July 2008, Merrill Lynch managed to lose $52 million every day, for a total of $19.2 billion, and somehow stayed in business. But if you looked at the yang to that yin, from 1999 to 2008 Lehman Brothers grew from $2.7 billion to over $19 billion, so how bad could it be?

I hit more stores for furniture for my booth, but it's all too big or too expensive or way too heavy to ship. Am I reinventing the wheel here? Is there not standard stuff that everyone uses since going to trade shows is what all companies do? I can't believe how friggin' hard this little detail is proving to be.

I've decided that instead of having banners with photos on them, I'll make posters of my gorgeous photos mounted on foam core, because the banners seem to destroy the quality of the photos. Near the print shop I find myself at a Pier 1 Imports (a blast from the past) and voilà, there's furniture I can use for the trade show. I find a cute little white table that I can write orders on, and a table stand for displaying my brochures. The items aren't too heavy, and they're priced reasonably. Finally!

There's still so much to figure out about the website. The web design company wants me to give them all the copy for the site, explaining how blankyclip works and why people need it. "You know the product best, so it's best if you write it," my designer tells me. I'd envisioned the company doing the snazzy writing, but I keep learning the same lesson that it all comes down to me. Am I qualified for the job of being me?

I meet with a friend who has a business selling makeup online at a discount. He shows me how he boxes up his merchandise, weighs it, and prints out his UPS shipping labels. I feel the heart palpitations again. UPS labels? Now I need UPS labels? He tells me that he has different pricing structures, and all this information is on his website. He's put it in the coding. "Will that be in your coding?" he asks.

He's arrived at his shipping price based on how much people are buying, not so much on where the order is shipping. "But you should be careful, because if someone orders from Hawaii you can really get screwed with the shipping costs," he warns. Someone is going to order blankyclips from Hawaii and screw me with shipping costs? More to worry about. I notice the different sizes of boxes he has, all very organized, and I wonder where my boxes will go. I ask him where I can buy the boxes and a scale to weigh them. He sends me to Box City in Pasadena, which sells boxes of every dimension you can imagine. I walk the aisles in amazement. They have everything, including the tape and the tape gun (why are they always guns?) and the plastic bags to put the product into before it is boxed up. If only I knew which sizes I'll need.

Still July 2008. We're screaming toward the trade show, just two months away. I have furniture for my booth, marketing materials, ribbon, everything I'm going to need—except the product I'm going to sell. This mama needs her blankyclips, so I meet with my Orthodox manufacturing guys. I tell them I've had an epiphany: I need to head back to China to oversee the start of the manufacturing run. If I learned anything from that last visit, it's that I better be there to make sure things go right. This is a huge order for me, 10,000 units, and I'll need to bring back some product for the upcoming trade show. At this point I would never receive the shipment in time, and I can't exactly have a booth without product to show. The Orthodox guys tell me that when I bring back some of the order, I have to make sure they're labeled samples or else they can be confiscated. The U.S. Customs people don't want goods brought in that aren't paid for in the proper way if they're intended for sale. "You don't need to worry, although there might be dogs at the airport sniffing your suitcases," one of the guys tells me. Excuse me? I go straight to panic. I picture trained blankyclip-sniffing dogs snarling at me as I'm hauled off to jail.

Before I return to China to kick off the blankyclip run, I meet with Paul, who's come over to discuss painting some cardboard boxes I want to use as display pieces for my booth. I have this idea of painting different-sized boxes as if they were baby blocks and putting my company logo on the sides. Pretty cute and clever, I think. I found Paul on Craigslist as a mural painter, and he says he's never painted on cardboard but thinks it should work out fine. He has to rush the job for me, though, as he's being deployed back to Afghanistan. Paul the painter is also a soldier in the National Guard. It's his second tour there, and he's not excited about it. Painting is his passion. I remember the woman I met in Dallas in the post office line, her life upended by Hurricane Katrina, and I'm glad to be able to make the small gesture of hiring Paul before he has to go. I watch him load my boxes into his old Sierra pickup, and I pray no harm will come to him.

FORTUNE 400,000 UNEMPLOYED

General Motors announced the layoffs of 34,000 people this year. GM blamed the layoffs on the $1 billion in losses it suffered *each month* from September 2007 to March 2008. 34,000 layoffs at GM and 73,000 at Citigroup and 25,000 at Hewlett-Packard and 17,000 at AT&T and 8,500 at American Airlines—that came to 400,000 people who would lose their jobs in 2008 (not the total number, by the way—that was only at twenty companies).

I meet with the owner of a baby boutique in my neighborhood to revisit the pricing question. I'm hoping I'll get reinforcement that $48, the figure suggested by the buyer at the Juvenile Shop, is the right price for my gift set. I've been taking Dagny to the music classes the owner offers in the back of his store, so I have a relationship with him. It's the perfect place to sell blankyclips, as he carries high-end merchandise, and I'm not surprised when he tells me that he loves my product and thinks it will do well. However, I am surprised when he tells me that he can't carry it in his store. "We're eco-friendly. Your blanket is not cotton, and we only sell green items," he proudly proclaims. He also tells me that they don't price their items at 2x wholesale but at 2.2x wholesale. So even if he did sell my non-green blankyclips and blanket, he'd have to overcharge or I'd have to sell to him at a discount.

He goes on to tell me, "Most of the products in this store are here on consignment, and we're not doing well in the retail department, actually, so if you'd like to think about putting a couple in the store for free, I could see how well they sell." For free? I'm flabbergasted. So, he won't sell blankyclips in his store if I *charge* him for them, but he will sell them in his store if I *give* them to him? And if I don't charge him for them, does it matter if they're cotton or polyester or made out of asbestos? Does he know how much money I'm in for by now? Money is the whole point, mister, and I'm not planning on giving this stuff to stores for free to see if they sell or not. That's insane. I try not to let on that I think he's insane, as I still want to keep taking the music classes with my daughter, but I certainly feel differently about the products he's selling, knowing that he hasn't paid for most of what is on his shelves. And wait, what was that about his retail sales not doing well?

A BANK YOU'VE NEVER HEARD OF EVAPORATES

July 2008. IndyMac disappeared. Earlier this month, their stock—which had traded at $50 a share in 2006—closed at $0.31. Yes, that was thirty-one cents. IndyMac tried cutting 3,800 jobs to keep things going, but even with $32 billion in assets, IndyMac ceased to exist, one of the largest bank failures in the history of the United States. And it just happened. Just now. Hello? Anyone paying attention out there?

Never mind, I have a company to launch. In order to get my registered number from the FTC, I have to send them a sample of each clip. All plush toys have this number, I discovered way back when. I'm still amazed that my manufacturing guys haven't told me to get this or any other info for my labeling. I'm on my own, no doubt about that. I don't think Ms. Fisher and Mr. Price have these issues when they launch a new product. I need to get this registered number in time for the factory to print the labels, which will then get sewn into the blankyclips.

TIME TO BE FRANK

Mid-July 2008. Congressman Barney Frank said—in spite of the fact that U.S. banks heavily invested in mortgage-backed securities (whatever the heck those were) *lost $435 billion*—that the future prospects of Fannie Mae and Freddie Mac were "solid."

Two friends who are also original investors have agreed to come to Las Vegas for part of the week to help work the booth. Gary will help as well. The days will be long, and I certainly couldn't be there without him. So that's four bodies that I'd like to clothe in a nice shirt that represents the company. I meet with a great guy from Big 10 Productions and order twelve light blue polo shirts, as we can't wear the same shirt for five days. We'll have these shirts for all the future shows we'll attend, and they'll give my company a professional look. The blankyclip logo will be on the upper front. They're going to look amazing. I'm excited.

I'm on my way to meet Megan, who's with a company my husband used to work for. (He's moved on, yet again. From makeup to backpacks.) She's in the PR department and thinks she can help me create a press kit for The blankyclip Company, Inc. I need professionally written press releases, company bio sheets, etc., to bring to the trade show. As I'm sitting at a traffic light, I feel my car sway as if it's been hit. It's the weirdest feeling, and I have no idea what has made my car move, as it's not windy at all. I make eye contact with the driver on my right, and he nods his head as if to say, "Yeah, I felt that too." What we don't know is that a 5.5 magnitude earthquake has just occurred in Chino Hills, twenty-eight miles away. It's the strongest earthquake to hit the Los Angeles area since the 1994 Northridge quake. Thankfully, Eli doesn't feel it while playing outside at his preschool, and Dagny and her babysitter are also oblivious while playing at the park.

I join her with my tea only to find out Megan is planning her wedding and is not at all available. She is here to give me the name of a friend, Ashley, who works at a theater company and freelances on the side. I don't have the money to hire most people who do this kind of thing, so I need a little miracle once again. Not only do I need to create a press kit, but I also need to make 400 copies and have them shipped to Las Vegas in time for the different media outlets that come to scout early.

Hard to believe I am asking for quotes on shipping my booth

items to Las Vegas. I need to figure out how many boxes I'll be shipping and their dimensions, and then the shipping company will come to my house to pick them up and ship them right to the area where my booth is! It's all getting very real and very scary. It would be so nice if by now I had the product I'm displaying.

With all the problems last time of not having my Blackberry work correctly in China, I'm being proactive about calling Verizon to get it all sorted out for this next trip. They assure me that I should have no problems.

My ribbon guy, George, is making me a label with just the word blankyclip on it. I can't believe I almost had the product made without a clear presentation of the blankyclip name. But now the factory is going to sew a label onto each blankyclip so that it will be easy to spot the name. It's easier to have George print these up for me—10,000 of them—and bring them to China than try to explain to the factory what I want. Since they're only about an inch long, all 10,000 fit easily into a gallon Ziploc bag. George also has a hang tag ready for me to approve, and I do approve! The cardstock is perfect, and the colors are beautiful. I love these moments of delight over a hang tag.

LET THE GOOD TIMES ROLL . . . AWAY

In August 2008, Bank of America stock traded at $29.31. It was $46.54 two years ago. To show they were responsible businessmen, Bank of America announced 35,000 layoffs. They also snapped up the Countrywide mortgage business for $2.5 billion, which six years later would blossom to a $52 billion loss.

August 2008. Time again to file an Extension Request for my trademark, since I'm still not selling blankyclips. It's my fifth Extension Request, and the last one allowed. I've got six more months to start selling my product. Happily, the trade show's around the corner . . .

I fill out a contract at a Public Storage facility where I've reserved a space for the blankyclips and the blankets. As much as we organized the home garage, I don't have room to house 10,000 blankyclips and 5,000 blankets. The storage facility is giving me the first month free. I have to get my own lock, but otherwise I'm all set.

Tonight, I fly to China for the blankyclip production run. This time I decide to stay in Shenzhen and avoid the two or three hours of travel each way every day. I'm staying at the Sheraton, which the Orthodox guys recommended. Once the clips are made, I'll end the trip in Hong Kong. This time the flight feels long, and I am not as jubilant to have hours and hours to myself. I already miss Gary and the kids.

Shenzhen doesn't feel like the same city that my factory's in when I'm sitting in a fancy-shmancy hotel with chandeliers in the lobby and marble everywhere. How is it that my factory is just minutes away on a dirt road, with a hole in the floor to pee in? I have the afternoon to settle in, but I'm not going anywhere because I'm completely absorbed in reading *A New Earth* by Eckhart Tolle and watching, on my tiny iPod, the Oprah interviews with him between each chapter. I'm taking much comfort from their conversations about how we react to what life hands us. So the afternoon flies by, and before I know it I'm having dinner and then channel surfing before bed.

The next day, Peter picks me up in the lobby to take me to the factory. The factory owner is driving, and he doesn't look happy to see me. Has time not healed old wounds? At the factory, he shows me why he's not happy. He's run into trouble with the brown fabric I chose for the bear clips. The "trouble": he doesn't actually have the brown fabric.

In case you missed it, I've flown from Los Angeles to begin the production run for the 10,000 clips that I will begin selling at my first trade show in Las Vegas in a matter of weeks, and he doesn't have the fabric I picked out on my previous visit six weeks ago. Through Peter, he explains that the truck that was driving the brown bear fabric down to Shenzhen from northern China has had some problems and has not arrived. He hopes it will arrive the next day. Or the day after.

"I thought it was coming from the fabric stall where I picked out what fabric I wanted," I say in my calmest voice.

"No, they ran out," Peter tells me. "He had to order it from the factory that makes it, and then he ran into those problems with the truck."

I'm sure the factory owner knows how big of a problem this is, and the way he handles it is to not be around me much. Unapologetically scattered about in huge boxes are thousands of little empty duck blankyclips casings. The boxes are open and the windows are open and the place is quite dirty, which makes me wonder how we are keeping my product clean, but there's no one to ask or complain to, so I just have to bear it. I'm accompanied by Peter and a new addition, BK, who speaks some English and often works with my Orthodox guys as their Quality Control man. They have recommended that I hire him for this purpose. They say it will save me lots of hassle and money, as BK will make sure that the factory is making my product as I intend for them to make it. BK asks me lots of questions and studies the three blankyclips and takes lots of notes. Good, finally someone who seems to care as much as I do.

I'd imagined that the whole factory would be manufacturing blankyclips once I arrived and that it'd be just a crazy hustle and bustle of blankyclips everywhere. Like most of my assumptions, this one is wrong too. The factory workers are working on quite a few other projects. One or two people seem to be working on my product. Mostly, there are pieces of clips and foam padding and fabric scattered about and the factory owners are ignoring me and there doesn't seem to be much production happening at all, but there is a whole lot of smoking and drinking tea going on in the little office room.

The day ends, and I've managed to forgo any meals, so I'm eager to get to my hotel and have dinner. Also, I have a date with Eckhart and Oprah as they talk about how to handle what life throws at us. Perfect timing, because life is throwing a lot of crap at me that seems beyond my control. I find a charming Italian restaurant in the hotel, and I sit with my iPod and my pasta dinner (quite delicious), but listening to Eckhart and Oprah is what is really feeding me.

I wake up the next morning to discover that a typhoon has moved into Shenzhen and it's too dangerous to go to the factory today. Naturally. So, I'm stuck in the hotel, and I'm not overseeing the production of 10,000 blankyclips. Instead, I'm enjoying the breakfast buffet (also quite delicious) and reading. Then BK finds me and asks if I want to go next door to the mall to do some shopping. Well, why not? The one-minute walk is a bit harrowing in the bad weather, but now I can add being in a typhoon to my list of things I didn't expect to happen on my trip. There's a huge toy store in the mall, and I'm curious about what a toy store in China looks like and what toys are being sold. I find a plastic ball that changes its colors when you throw it and the plastic pieces rearrange themselves. Pretty cool, so I grab two for my kids. I am intrigued by some cute stuffed animals that are made to hang on a window, with suction cups attached to short strings; I get one in pink and one in blue. I have to get a few Beijing Olympics washcloths for the kids, even though I won't be anywhere near the Olympics. The signs are everywhere for the upcoming games, and it's definitely neat to be in China before such a monumental event.

Back at the hotel, we're hanging out in the lobby discussing the next day's schedule when we hear a thunderous crash. One of the fancy giant panels of glass that hangs in the front lobby, about fifteen feet tall, has fallen! Apparently, the fancy Western-style hotel is held together by shoestrings. Shattered glass is everywhere, but no one is hurt, and no one seems too concerned. I guess when there's no one to sue, it's not that much of a problem.

CLIPPED

The next day, the typhoon passes. I head to the pool to swim some laps before a long day at the factory. It's a huge clover-shaped pool with not a soul in sight. As I swim, I start to freak myself out about what might be in the pool water, considering that there are so many factories around spewing God knows what waste. I wonder why I'm the only person here. Does everyone else know something I don't know? Could I get sick swimming in water that I'm not supposed to drink? Do they use chlorine to keep the water clean, or some other chemical that hasn't been approved "for birth and up"? I get more and more anxious as I swim, which causes the reverse effect that I was going for. And as I hover on the edge of the pool, there's suddenly a hotel employee in uniform squatting down to tell me something. I hear her say, "You have black face?" and I'm terrified. I think that the pool chemicals have darkened my face. "I have a black face?" I say back to her, as I jump out of the pool and grab my towel. "You have black face?" she repeats, but this time she mimes eating, and I understand her to be asking me if I've had breakfast. I'm being asked by a customer-service-oriented and friendly member of the waitstaff if I have eaten yet. I want to laugh out loud, but the joke would be lost, and I realize I'm a paranoid crazy woman. So much for exercise.

Peter picks me up, and we drive to the factory where I'm feeling unwanted. But miracle of miracles, the brown fabric has arrived. It's not the same brown fabric I picked out six weeks ago, but it's actually nicer, so everyone is smiley and getting along. Then I study some of the sheep blankyclips that have been assembled, and I'm unhappy with how the white fuzzy fabric looks on the arms and legs. There are areas that seem to be missing some fuzz where you can see through to the backing of the fabric. I point this out to the factory owner, and I can see how angry he is with me. He grabs an end of the fabric to show me that when it's in a huge roll you can't tell that some areas are less fuzzy until you cut a small piece. There's nothing he can do about that, and this is the fabric I chose. He's right, and I see it's not something we can change at this point. I just hope I'm being overly critical and it's not something people will notice.

There are enough completed animal body casings to begin the process of inserting the foam-padded clip. The factory owner sits down at a table in the workroom with a huge bag of uncovered clips, a roll of foam, and some glue. He figures out the best way to glue the foam onto the plastic clip. (Didn't we already take care of this?) A few women are stuffing filling into the bellies of the animal bodies, grabbing little bits of a different, softer foam from an enormous bag. They chat and stuff bellies. It all feels dreadfully slow and small to me. I'd imagined the whole factory would be working on my product, but most of the young workers are completing some giant order that's shipping to Italy. The factory owner is excited about that job as it's way bigger than my measly 10,000 blankyclips. In China, a country with over 1.3 billion people, 10,000 anything is peanuts.

I spend most of the morning sitting in the office waiting for something to happen. Peter and BK tell me that we're going to a nearby restaurant for lunch. We walk down the four flights out onto the dirt road, crowded with people. I see a woman with a baby strapped to her back by a cloth, its little tush exposed. I quickly see why when the baby begins to poop. The woman doesn't miss a step, and no one's concerned about baby poop falling onto the dirt road. Nowhere in sight are diapers, strollers, or anything that would make a product like a blankyclip even remotely necessary, yet I'm here to manufacture them. If the meaning of irony is a state of affairs that seems contrary to what one expects and is often amusing as a result, then I am knee-deep in irony.

The afternoon trudges along, with only a handful of workers assigned to building blankyclips. BK, my quality controller, is mostly chatting in the office, but occasionally he goes out to the workroom to inspect a blankyclip. He finds one that has a defect—a hole in one of the seams—and makes sure I'm aware of his discovery.

It's the end of the day, and I'm on the two-hour train ride to Hong Kong. I'm staying in the same hotel, but my arrival is so different from when I stayed there six weeks ago and could barely move from exhaustion. Now I check in like a pro and zip up to my room.

The factory owner told me that for this last day there's no reason for me to be in the factory, as they just need to get the clips done. I'd told him even before arriving that I'd need to leave with 100 blankyclips in my suitcase. The trade show in Las Vegas is in less than a month, and the shipment of 10,000 blankyclips will not make it by then. I'm now in Hong Kong, and this is my last day, and I don't have 100 blankyclips with me. Peter says he'll pick them up from the factory later today and bring them to me at my hotel in Hong Kong.

Hong Kong is having a huge downpour. I go out anyway, to keep my mind off the panic that I possibly won't be seeing those 100 blankyclips before I board my plane tomorrow morning. My Blackberry is in a pocket of my yellow raincoat in case Peter calls to let me know he's arrived with the blankyclips. I go in and out of shops and try on clothes that are too expensive and end up in a supermarket where I get the kids some little toy instruments, chocolate, and beaded pouches that are only a few dollars.

About the middle of the day, I notice that my raincoat is drenched. I check the pocket with the phone. The buttons have locked, and I can't even unlock the screen to dial out. The phone is dead. I have no way for Peter to reach me. I head back to the hotel, call Los Angeles from my room, and thankfully reach one of my Orthodox guys. I tell him what's happened with my phone and ask him to please use the hotel number to leave me messages, and to give Peter that information as well. It is such a relief when the phone rings in my hotel room a little later and it's Peter. He tells me, "They're still working on the hundred pieces. I'll be at your hotel at ten tonight, since they won't be ready before then."

I'm leaving in the morning. Flying back to Los Angeles. If I don't have these 100 blankyclips, then my trip here to make sure that my product was manufactured correctly, and to bring back the samples I'll need to launch my business at the biggest baby-product trade show in the country, will be a complete bust. I'm alone and have no one to talk to, so I keep listening to Eckhart and Oprah. How I react to things does not change them. I keep reading and watching and reading and watching the chapter interviews.

In the movie version of my life, we would be staring at the hands on a big clock. At 10:00 p.m., Peter arrives with a cardboard box full of blankyclips. We meet in the lobby to do the handoff. He opens up the box and pulls out a blankyclip for me. I'm overjoyed that they actually finished these 100 clips. That is, until I check one and work the mechanism (i.e., squeeze it open, like my quality control guy should've done) to discover that the clip squeaks. It's freakin' squeaking, a really annoying sound of metal on metal. What the hell did they do to my product?

At this point, I have a kind of out-of-body-experience. In a nanosecond, I decide that I must become the hysterical business-woman who's been wronged and who's furious and who must be dealt with. After listening to Eckhart all week, I know that being hysterical isn't going to change what happened and that I need not act that way, but at the same time I realize that if I don't, I'm never going to get this huge screwup fixed. So, while I'm aware of an unnatural internal calm, I embrace the role of hysterical woman. Peter calls the factory owner immediately.

They have no idea why the clip is squeaking. The factory owner knows that the prototype I approved did not have a squeak. Peter holds a blankyclip up to his phone so the factory owner can hear the squeak. It's one of those squeaks you'd slap WD-40 on if you heard it on a hinge. The factory owner assumes that the inner metal coil was tightened too much. They will all have to be redone. It's agreed that Peter will head back to the factory and the owner will get some workers to come in and fix the 100 pieces so that I can have them in the morning. I continue to be hysterical so that Peter understands how vital this is. People walk past us in the lobby and stare. A little girl approaches us and wants to hold one of the blankyclips. I remain hysterical, but I'm secretly pleased to see that she's drawn to the duck clip and wants to play with it.

I have been in China for five days, and I'm leaving in the morning. I'm going to bed without 100 finished blankyclips in my possession. Somehow, I'm supposed to sleep?

In the morning, Peter calls. "I'm not going to be able to bring the product to your hotel, but I'll meet you at the airport," he says. There's nothing I can do when he tells me this. I hope he really does intend to meet me there. I really hope that he'll have the 100 blankyclips with him. Mostly, I really hope that there was a point to getting a bank loan, a patent, a photographer, a designer, a booth, a . . . and putting myself through all of this.

My plan is to pack most of the 100 "samples" in my suitcase and some in my carry-on bag. I'm at the airport waiting with bated breath when I see Peter carrying a box. He is walking in slow motion and the wind is blowing his hair back. Actually, he is rushing over to me, and he looks exhausted. He tells me that they finished at three in the morning. The 100 clips don't squeak, and they look absolutely amazing! I'm so relieved I could scream, but I'm in the airport of a Communist country, so I don't.

Eli loved holding Mama's blankyclip prototypes. He's all dressed up for this photo shoot. The close-up shot on his baby fingers shows how safe, padded, and loosely tensioned the clips are.

Prototypes, before the cute animals were added, on Eli's stroller over one of his blankets. Taken on the sly in a botanical garden, showing how the clips go over the sunshade and the food tray below.

The entrance to the factory where blankyclips were made.

The bathroom in the factory. I took a good guess how to use it.

Factory workers in the front are making blankyclips,
assembling the inner clips and stuffing the animals' bellies

My master shot of duck blankyclips and the ecru blanket on a stroller.
From the photo shoot for my packaging and marketing.

The awesome shot we got of Dagny holding a sheep blankyclip,
right after she had a toddler tantrum.
Ended up being a very important shot for my marketing!

Dagny in a double stroller, playing with a sheep blankyclip.
Meanwhile, two bears are helping her "sibling" sleep next-door.

Baby sleeping in a bouncy seat with bear blankyclips and a blanket to keep her cozy. This was the understudy baby who did a fantastic job sleeping, so we could get this amazing shot.

The three designs of blankyclips—sheep, duck, and bear—with their blankets, packaged for the boutiques.
The blankets are rolled and held together with ribbon.

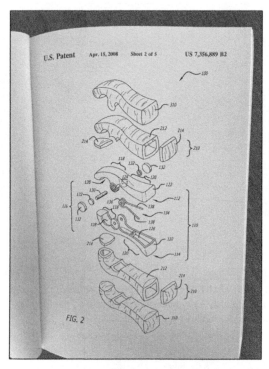

FIG. 2

The exploded view drawing of my invention to show exactly how it is put together. All patents require very specific drawings, showing how the invention is assembled and how it works.

I'm in the booth we set up for the Las Vegas JPMA trade show, with the boxes I hired a painter to make. I'm very happy to have figured out how to set it all up and display blankyclips.

In our duplex with the blankyclip order, moments before it was shipped to thirty Buy Buy Baby stores.

The three designs of blankyclips hanging in a Buy Buy Baby store.

Gary and I shooting a blankyclip video with Eli and Dagny playing "blankyclip superheroes!" They arrive to save a "mom" (another little girl) whose blanket has fallen off her stroller.
We had so much fun making these videos with our kids.

A mock-up for the last packaging that never was produced.
It was made to hold two blankyclips, without the blanket,
to sell at a lower price point.

7

What Doesn't Happen in Vegas

August 2008. Back home. Less than a month until the trade show and so much still to get done.

It's so wonderful to be home with my family and to watch my two kids playing together on their foam alphabet mat in the living room. Then the whole family is suddenly off to Glendale Memorial Hospital. Dagny, my leftie, seems to have turned into a rightie and is no longer using her left arm at all. That arm is just hanging by her side. At the hospital we discover that she has nursemaid's elbow, which comes from lifting a child by the hands (her father was getting her off a chair) and pulling the elbow joint out of its socket. It's why you're not supposed to swing kids in the air by their arms. Sockets are pretty loose at one and three-quarter years of age.

Dagny is on my lap as the doctor bends her arm forward and does this fast kamikaze move to twist her elbow back into place. This is called a reduction. She screams, as he backs off and says, "Now watch how quickly she'll go back to using her left hand." Within minutes she's using her left hand naturally and acting as if there was no reason for our visit. I'm incredibly relieved but now wondering if this is my punishment for being away for seven days. Thank goodness I wasn't gone longer. Gary admits he really didn't notice anything was wrong. I decide to continue to love him because there are lots of other things he got right while I was away. It's myself I'm on the fence about.

I meet Ashley, my PR help-for-hire, for lunch. She shows me the gorgeous press releases she's written about my business, a bio page about me, and a great "here's what you can say about blankyclips" page to entice press folks to write about me and my company. She's also put it all on a disc, and she encourages me to get the whole press kit copied on discs since most magazines will only take material electronically these days. I'm feeling very legit. Now I need to make 400 copies of everything as suggested by the trade show media department.

I run to my Orthodox guys to relay the details they don't already know about my China trip. They tell me the product looks amazing and that I've done great work by going over there twice. They aren't too surprised to hear about all the issues I ran into. They've been manufacturing in China for many years and know how it goes. But I think they're impressed with the fact that I've handled this on my own. I'm sure they weren't expecting a woman—I mean, we can get pregnant!—to do what I did. To be fair, I wasn't expecting me to do it on my own either.

Today, the blankets I've had manufactured are delivered right to my Public Storage unit, 129 boxes of blue, ecru, and pink baby blankets that I'll sell with blankyclips. Gift sets, here we come!

The truck is a broken-down old postal truck, and the driver is about 100 years old. The first challenge that presents itself is that the back of his truck doesn't seem to want to lower—the lowering mechanism thingy's stuck. He finds a metal bar and bangs the crap out of the joint that isn't moving. Eventually, all his whacking gets the thingy unstuck, and he's able to put a whole stack of boxes on a pallet with wheels. The whole process is grueling to watch, as this man is really too old for this kind of work, but bit by bit he takes the boxes to the storage unit and stacks them by color. Back and forth from the truck to the storage unit he goes, and it's a hot day. I watch him get sweatier and sweatier, but he's in awfully good spirits, considering. Eventually all 129 blanket boxes are stacked neatly in my storage unit. I'm not exactly sure how all the blankyclip boxes are going to fit in here as well, but I'll deal with that when I need to. At this point, it feels miraculous that 5,000 blankets I'm going to sell are all sitting patiently in a hot storage facility in Glendale, California.

Time to talk to Bank of America to set up my Merchant Services. I need to be able to take credit card payments on my website. Bank of America will run the order through, but Authorize.net will collect the funds. It's complicated, and somewhere in the recesses of my mind I recall my plan to license my idea to a company and collect royalties, but this will be how I'm able to process orders on my website and collect revenue. Let's pray there will be many such orders.

The photo display to hang at the back of my booth is ready at the printer. The logo looks great, and the images are beautiful. I'm nervous about getting them banged up, so we bubble-wrap the bazoozies out of them. I've invited Patty and her new business partner over for pizza dinner with the kids. She's been doing so much for my company and has barely been charging me for her services. I'm incredibly grateful for her support and can't wait until I'm in a position to pay her well. I know she's barely out of college, but she's so talented and hardworking and reliable.

The shipping company arrives to pick up my eighteen boxes that are going to Las Vegas. Everything has been labeled very specifically so they can bring it all inside the convention center and deliver it right to my booth at the trade show. It's a relief to have these boxes out of my life now, or at least my home. Thank goodness Gary will be with me and will help me set it all up. The next daunting thought, but let me at least enjoy this moment!

September 2008. To Vegas at last! In my packed-to-the-gills car, I have luggage, blankyclips, and all the things that didn't get shipped a week or so ago. And my two kids. Gary has more luggage in his car, along with our babysitter and her teenage daughter, who will watch our kids all week and keep them entertained while we're working the trade show. We make lots of stops to stretch legs and pee, and to keep an almost five-year-old and an almost two-year-old from going crazy on a long car ride. It seemed the easiest option to bring the kids. I wasn't about to leave them in LA, so far away, for a week, and I want to keep tabs on those elbows this time.

We pull into the hotel check-in lane safe and sound—270 miles through the desert is no picnic. Just then Dagny explodes a giant diarrhea-esque poo through her diaper. Apparently, the strawberry milk from Subway didn't agree with her tummy. I'll say. I take her into the lobby bathroom and do my best to clean her up on the counter, as there is no changing table. Her clothes are trashed, and that is where they end up. I blow through all my baby wipes and a stack of rough brown paper towels. This isn't exactly the most fortuitous way to begin the trade show as the owner of a small business about to launch a product she's worked on for the past five years. Covered in shit.

Today is booth setup day! It's fun seeing all the different booths getting assembled. Also nerve-wracking. These people clearly have the trade show thing down. I see polished-looking booths coming together, and suddenly the boxes painted with my logo look juvenile and the beautiful, giant hanging photos seem ridiculously hard to hang. I see people with great displays on portable stands that seem easy to travel with and (most importantly) are made to be used over and over again.

Mine was a shipping nightmare. But we get the photos hung and start building forward. The boxes need to be taped closed. They seem too big for the space, so we have to rethink where they'll go. I feel disheartened and unprepared. Lovingly, Gary keeps me encouraged, and we keep unpacking. There are too many painted boxes, so we stow some of the smaller ones inside the bigger ones. We put the little white table and chair in a corner and fill the little drawer with the credit card swiper and some order forms and pens.

The bouncy seat is on display with a blue blanket secured by two bear blankyclips, and the Peg Perego stroller has a pink blanket on it with the different blankyclips on various parts of the stroller. It's all coming together in a cute way, and I've cycled around to thinking that my booth looks warm and inviting. I display the three gift set options on the furry sheepskin rug I picked up for my photo shoot, and they look great. There are loose blankyclips in a wicker basket so people can pick them up and see how they work.

The hanging photo display that shows how to use a blankyclip is critical, but since this is a new product that people haven't seen before—and truly they've not seen anything remotely like it—it's going to take lots of hands-on selling. My booth is in the New Products section, and I've heard that the buyers really like to check out what's new. I've also paid a fee to display blankyclip in a special area featuring only a select few products, so that after buyers see it there in a glass case, they can come find my booth to check it out. On top of that, I'm a finalist for the New Products Award from the Juvenile Products Manufacturers Association. They'll announce the winner during the week. More I cannot do.

Time to pick up the Leads Retrieval System that I rented for the show. This is a little device that tracks any leads you may get. You use it to scan people's badges so that their info is uploaded electronically. At the end of the show, they give you a file with all the info about who has come to visit your booth in case you don't get everyone's business card. Our badges all have a chip in them that can be read only by this scanner. Very fancy. We have to wear these badges around our necks to go in and out of the trade show, and it's a thrill to see our names on a badge that says "The blankyclip Company, Inc." and "ABC Kids Expo."

It's been a long day, but now it's time to see the kids. They show us the stuffed animals they have acquired during a fruitful day at Circus Circus. Our dinner with them is brief because Gary and I are going to see *O* by Cirque du Soleil at the Bellagio, a longtime dream of mine. The kids are a bit put out that we're leaving them again, and more than a bit indifferent to the fact that Mommy is finally getting to see this inventive show, but it's their bedtime and we have a babysitter.

September 7, 2008. Today the trade show begins! It's also our twelfth wedding anniversary, so it's a very meaningful day. My friend and blankyclip investor, Sean, arrives to help man the booth. In his blankyclip-logoed blue polo shirt and his khakis and his badge, he looks very official. Sean is great at talking to people and selling an idea, so his contribution will be huge. I feel anxious, but I'm ready to sell some blankyclips! Hanging in the lobby right by the main entrance to the trade show is an enormous banner that lists the Pearl Sponsors, and my company's logo is right there for all to see. Yes, I paid to be a Pearl Sponsor. I want as much publicity as I can get.

It's not all that busy, and by that I mean we don't get too many buyers walking past our booth. And by that I mean it's very slow. When buyers do walk by, they seem to be taking our booth in with their peripheral vision, like they don't want to make eye contact and actually hear about our product. Boredom sets in, and we decide to take turns walking around ourselves to see what's going on in the rest of the show.

Wow. A lot is going on in the rest of the show! But where a lot is going on is in the giant booths of Fisher-Price and Carter's and Disney. Almost nothing is going on in the little start-ups and new small businesses. There's buzz that today is slow, but it will pick up. Everyone waits for the buyers to arrive, and some of the small businesses are pissed. We were promised a big turnout of buyers from all over the country. I don't have other trade shows to compare this one with, but it's a relief to hear that I'm not the only one feeling unnoticed here.

After we've taken turns doing the rounds and seeing what's going on in other rows of booths, we begin to reach out to the booths in our own row. There's a comforter company, a cloth diaper company, a teething necklace company, and a backpack company. These people have come here from all over the country and are at different stages in their businesses. Most have been selling on a small scale and have come to get into the big chains, or at least the medium-sized chains. I notice that their booths could fit in the back of a car, and that they've come up with much lighter ways of displaying their products. I seem to be the only one in my row who's sent so many boxes with the shipping company. One young couple tells me that they've purchased furniture for their display at a nearby Kmart and will return it after the show. Others have figured out how to use the cases or boxes they store their items in as the display pieces as well. How did I not think of this?

My boothmates and I develop strategies to get people to talk to us. As attendees walk down the aisle, we try to figure out from their badges if they're here to display, like we are, and are on a boredom pass around the show, or if they're indeed buyers from a store that might carry our product. If they're buyers, we step out into their path with a blankyclip and just begin talking to them about it. Waiting for them to show an interest in us hasn't been working, so we have to be more aggressive. Some buyers seem to be okay with this strategy, but others are put off. I don't understand why buyers would walk down our aisle and not even look at our booth. How have they surmised that my product is not for them? Why not meet us? Isn't that why they're walking down the aisle of the New Products section? They came to Vegas to *not* see new products?

The day ends with no sales. We've spoken mostly with other small business owners who are here to sell their products, and the consensus is that the day was slow but things will pick up as the week goes on. We go back to the hotel room, and the kids are very happy to see us. Their day has been much more exciting, apparently, as they've won more stuffed animals from the carnival games at Circus Circus. I bathe them and put them to bed, and then we quietly sneak out (we've learned our lesson) to our anniversary dinner celebration. Delirious but committed.

Since September 7, 2008, is our twelfth wedding anniversary, not just the first day of the trade show, we sit next to a fake waterfall and toast these milestones. I am launching my exciting small business on such a special day.

UH, THIS CAN'T BE GOOD

September 7, 2008. Not just a nostalgic wedding anniversary, but also the day when the U.S. government took over Fannie Mae and Freddie Mac, causing a panic not completely unrelated to the lack of buyers at a Las Vegas baby trade show. While very few actual people were sure what Fannie and Freddie did, they watched a lot of talking heads shake those heads with a lot of concern. The takeover of Fannie Mae and Freddie Mac (officially, the Federal National Mortgage Association and the Federal Home Loan Mortgage Corporation) was described as one of the most sweeping government interventions ever in the private financial sector. Fannie Mae and Freddie Mac basically bought mortgages from banks and other lenders so those banks and other lenders would feel like being in the mortgage business was a good thing. Maybe it wasn't.

Day two of the trade show, and we're ready for action. There seem to be a few more buyers walking down our aisle, but not by much. Again, it's mostly other retailers checking out what we're selling. I get lots of positive feedback from them. It's amazing how many times I hear, "I wish there'd been a product like a blankyclip when I had kids, because my blanket was always falling off my stroller." It seems unanimous that the animal designs are adorable. Most of these exhibitors complain that their booths are dead too.

A buyer magically approaches my booth. "Can you sell the blankyclips individually without the blanket?" she asks. I tell her that at the moment I'm only selling them in a pair with a blanket, as a gift set. She says, "That's too bad because I would only want the clips."

I can't tell her that I have to bundle them with the blanket in order to get my pricing up where I need it since the cost of making the clips is high but the cost of making a blanket isn't. Instead, I say, "It's a great gift packaged all together!" She moves on.

I walk around the trade show on a break and stop at one of the big companies, Sunshine Kids. They have a humongous booth, and I know their product line. They were one of the companies I tried to license blankyclip to way back when.

The buyer files away an order form in a big stack of them. I tell her, "It's been very slow near my booth."

She confides, "These orders are coming from stores we're already doing business with. They're just putting in reorders. If I was waiting for new business, I'd have no orders to speak of." Uh oh. I'm here to launch a business, which *means* new orders.

My other investor friend, Ray, arrives tonight to help out in the booth for the next couple of days. I give him his light blue shirts, and we quickly fill him in on the blankyclip spiel. We now have a spiel, after two solid days under our belts. He's charismatic and unafraid to approach the buyers, and just as ready to dive in as Sean was. I'm not sure what I would do without these angels by my side.

Word the next day is that Target buyers are walking the floor. Target! Everyone in our row is all aflutter. We scour the badges that come down our aisle, but not a sign of Target anywhere. And then . . . could it be? A Target buyer is spotted a few rows down! Everyone is imagining the big order that would change everything. But this buyer never appears in our New Products row.

We do see a buyer from Carter's. He says, "My wife just had a baby and would probably really love having a blankyclip since we live in NYC and know all about blankets falling off strollers and getting dirty." I zap his info into my Leads Retrieval System, grab a blankyclip gift set, and nervously give it to him. He seems touched by the gesture. This little interaction gives us much to discuss for at least the next fifteen minutes of the trade show.

We get sillier and sillier as the day wears on. It's becoming clearer and clearer that the buyers just aren't buying much. The few that make it down our aisle don't seem to be from stores that would carry blankyclips. Another buyer asks me if I would sell the blankyclips individually, and I explain again, "Not at this moment, but the gift sets are great because everyone needs a blanket, and look how soft they are!" No thank you, and she walks away.

When a buyer from a store in Mexico comes by, my fluency in Spanish is a great help. She wants to know where I've manufactured the clips, and when I say China (*Verdad?*) she makes a face and puts the blankyclip back in the basket. I learn from her that Mexico currently has strict laws against selling products made in China, as they want to promote their own industry. She too asks if I'd sell the blankyclips without the blanket, and when I explain yet again they only come as a gift set, she tells me that Mexico is hot and my warm and fuzzy blankets are unnecessary there. She sees blankyclips as something people would pay a few dollars for in Mexico, and not as a $48 gift set. The people there don't have that kind of money. So this whole conversation is a big ol' bust amounting to nada.

We've made up a fun game, and here's how you play it. You take the stroller covered with the blanket attached by blankyclips, and then you slide it toward the booth across the aisle, trying to get as close to the booth as possible without going into it. It's like shuffleboard. The one who gets the stroller closest wins. We find this very entertaining, and soon others in our New Products row want to play too. It's better than sitting around calculating how much I've spent to be here and how little I seem to be getting back.

Day 4. The kids have had it with Vegas. They scream when I say goodbye, and they run out of the hotel room and chase me to the elevator. The babysitter runs after them, and it's a maniacal, horrible scene as the elevator doors close and my little girl reaches for me and screams, "NOOOO!" I'm trying hard to believe it makes sense that I'm leaving her for another long day at the trade show. Am I a fraud for trying to sell a product meant to help take care of a baby and yet my own baby is screaming for me to be with her?

Where is the onslaught of buyers predicted for the end of the week? People are unanimous in saying that last year's show was much better attended and that they've done much better at other shows (have I considered the gift trade shows?). I've had no orders, but I've taken many business cards and swiped many badges for follow-up after I get back home.

Today, there's interest from a Canadian buyer, and I learn that there are certain labeling requirements in order to sell plush toys in Canada. The buyer asks me if I could relabel my product to sell in Canada. Huh? I've just had my first production run, and the shipment is on its way from China, and no, I can't relabel my product. Really? Can I not have some interest from a store in the United States that is delighted to see I have been approved by ASTM F963 for birth and up? Just buy one, for the love of God!

Another buyer asks me about purchasing individual blankyclips. My booth cohorts think I should just break down and sell them individually. I can't imagine at what price this would make sense for me, or what price people would pay for a blankyclip or two. I've printed up my order forms, and they only show the gift set option. I don't have packaging for individual clips or a set of clips. If I don't sell my product with the blanket, I don't see how I can make enough on just the clips to put in a reorder.

And then it happens. The sweetest moment of the day comes when a buyer from a boutique in northern California sees my product and blithely says, "Sure, I'll put in an order for six." I'm so thrown by her interest that I have to pull myself together to fill out an order form. If I had let myself be stopped by all the no's along the way to this trade show (and certainly my daughter's "NO!" of this morning was the loudest), I would not be experiencing this overwhelming sense of pride. The buyer hands me a credit card and a sheet of paper that has all the info I'll be asking her for. I don't know what to do first. I must look like such a bozo filling out her order. She's in a rush, so she suggests that I grab her credit card info and keep the sheet, and she'll wait to hear from me with the total before I ship. I'm all smiles. Of course, I hope she doesn't suspect that she's my first actual order of the gift sets (wholesale at $24 per piece) I came here to sell. My trademark can now be official!

Once the buyer leaves our row, we take pictures of me holding the order form. There was a *yes!* Should I be in my booth sobbing with joy over one order?

I put the kids down that night and celebrate by . . . working on the blankyclip website. I can't believe it's not yet up and running, and we still have so many fixes to make. I'm so tired, but this has to get done. The buyers need to have a website to refer to after the show or I won't be taken seriously. How frustrating that I made it to this trade show, but my website did not.

Day 5. Last day of the show and also Gary's birthday. I'm sure the only present he really wants is to get the heck out of Vegas after this grueling week. We're running on fumes, and there's a frenzied energy running through the show. People are buying each other's samples and exchanging info. I'm sure Dagny will love the cow lunch bag I buy from the gals across the aisle. Her favorite lovey that she sleeps with every night is a cow named Boo. People are being much freer than they've been with whatever info they've acquired, so I'm getting buyers' contact info and names of stores to hit up. We've survived an exhausting week together in the New Products row, and a definite bond has been made.

Another sale! This buyer would like four of each design, so I'm giving her a thirteenth gift set for free, my Baker's Dozen special. When I ask for the name of her store, she tells me, "I sell strictly online and don't have a storefront." I hadn't thought about selling to an online-only business, but at this point I am much less choosy.

On this last day of the trade show, when a buyer from the posh baby store Bellini asks me if I'd be willing to sell her some individual blankyclips so she can take them back to Orange County, California, I'm game, believe you me. "I have to figure out a packaging solution, so give me some time. I'll call you in a little bit to come and pick them up," I tell her. She's agreed to buy a dozen blankyclips at a $7.50 wholesale price, to retail for $15 per clip. Amazing the role timing can play in a decision. How many others did I turn away before she asked?

The gals in the booth next to mine who've been selling little bands that say, "It's a boy!" or "It's a girl!" for a retail price of $2 each, help me tie my blankyclip ribbon around each clip so I can attach the hang tag to the bow. This isn't something I could've imagined doing on the first or second day of the trade show, but now it's a whole different story. And since the buyer is from a big company that has lots of stores all over the country, there is potential for this to turn into something big.

The buyer from Bellini Baby is delighted with how the ribbon looks on the individual clips and says she'll put them in a basket by the cash register at her store. She'll let me know how they sell. At 3:00 p.m. the show is declared over, and it's time to pack everything up. It's a madhouse suddenly as everyone is in a rush to get the hell out of here. Unfortunately, we have to wait for the shipping company to bring us our boxes. The folks who are throwing everything in the back of their cars or simply returning furniture to the nearby Kmart are moving fast. Many of the booths are empty already, and we are one of the slowest to leave. Yet another indication of being first-timers.

What an experience this trade show was! Despite the problems, I'm very glad I did it. It certainly was an important way to launch The blankyclip Co., Inc. I'm going to get contacts for all the buyers who came to the show and reach out to them. I'm going to do a big postcard mailing and just keep getting the word out about blankyclip. I expected to take more orders and to meet more buyers than I did, but everyone seems to agree that there were fewer buyers and less buying in general this year. Not sure why.

Three days after the trade show, on September 14, 2008, my bank was busy.

ASS(ET) MANAGEMENT

Bank of America acquired Merrill Lynch. Why? Because someone had to. Was Merrill Lynch too big to fail? Who would want to buy a company that lost $19.2 billion in the past year? The first of the 35,000 people set to lose their jobs because of the acquisition were shown the door. Within twenty-four hours, on September 15, 2008, Lehman Brothers filed for bankruptcy. On that day alone, the Dow Jones dropped 500 points. This 4.4% drop was the biggest decline for the Dow, percentage-wise, since July 2002.

I arrive in Los Angeles back from my very first trade show, and the Great Recession, the greatest global economic crisis since the Depression, arrives in all its glory too. What are the odds that I would be launching my company at the onset of the most devastating economic disaster of my lifetime?

Of course, I don't know any of this yet.

8

A Perfect Storm

NOW YOU SEE $8 TRILLION, NOW YOU DON'T

The Great Recession began when the housing bubble burst. All those mortgages that banks were in such a hurry to approve? In retrospect, maybe not such a brilliant idea. Because of mortgage defaults and the drop in real estate value, $8 TRILLION evaporated from the U.S. economy. That's a lot of money to disappear, and consumers reacted by spending less. That meant businesses earned less revenue because consumers were buying fewer goods and services. And the $8 trillion evaporation meant companies like Bear Stearns and Lehman Brothers disappeared, which scared the bejeezus out of the financial industry. So they put the brakes on business investment—at the very same time that businesses needed investment to offset the loss of consumer spending. Businesses reacted in the time-honored tradition of cutting expenses, and what's the highest-cost asset that businesses can cut? People. Lots of them. By the end of the Great Recession, that would be 8.4 million of them. September 2008 saw unemployment ratchet up to 6.1%, as compared to 4.7% one year earlier. And from August to September, overall retail sales in the United States plunged by $50 billion.

Still September 2008. I'm back in Los Angeles with some orders and a digital file full of leads. The economic landscape we've all been traversing for the past few years has apparently turned to quicksand. But I have utility patents, a storage shed full of blankets, and a factory in China to pull me out of the muck. And besides, for every doomsayer I hear projecting economic collapse, there's someone equally blind suggesting that these little downturns are cyclical and the holiday selling season will bring back prosperity. Everyone shops during the holidays, right? I have no other option than to be optimistic.

ALMOST TOO BIG TO FAIL
September 26, 2008. Washington Mutual, Inc., the largest savings and loan association in the United States, filed for Chapter 11 voluntary bankruptcy. WaMu had assets valued at $307 billion at the time of its failure. JPMorgan Chase bought WaMu's banking subsidiaries for $1.9 billion.

October 2008. My friend and investor Ray wants to help me sell blankyclips around his home in Palm Springs. He says, "There are lots of baby boutiques that I think will be interested." He's such a fan of the product and has so much enthusiasm. I need enthusiasm. Then I get an incredibly wonderful email from a buyer who has put in an order for twelve blankyclip gift sets! She was at the trade show, and she says that my product stood out as the most creative and unique product she saw.

NEW RECORD SET IN OCTOBER 2008!
The Conference Board announced that their Consumer Confidence Index was "at an all-time low." Oh, that kind of record. *All-time.* Economists shrugged and explained that that's what happens after a country loses 760,000 jobs in less than three months.

There's a local baby trade show coming up, and I have to decide if I can swing it. The smallest booth at Baby Celebration LA is $785. Ouch. But you can sell directly to the consumer, as it's open to the public, so it could be a great way to get the word out about my company. Building brand awareness is crucial at this point.

> **$785 IS A STARBUCKS RUN TO THE FINANCE INDUSTRY**
> The cost of the smallest booth at Baby Celebration LA was 0.0000001% of the $700 billion that the congressionally approved and presidentially executed Troubled Assets Relief Program (TARP) would be giving away.

I figure my assets are pretty troubled, so I look into the TARP program and see that the $700 billion is for the banks. Well, at least my bank will have more money to stick on my line of credit if I need it.

Betty, who works with the shipping company that's bringing my 9,900 blankyclips (I already took 100 home with me), calls me because there's a problem. "The shipment won't be released at the dock in Shenzhen because the factory hasn't drawn up the proper paperwork," she says. Here I've figured out how to manufacture a product in China, but now it's trapped there because of some piece of paper that the factory owner will not get to the right people? Help, Betty!

She calls back and tells me that she has sent someone to the factory. This mystery person has gotten the right paperwork from the owner, and the shipment can now be released from the customs/loading area. My blankyclips can now sail from China to California! They are due to leave on a vessel on October 12 and arrive in Long Beach on October 27. Bon voyage, my sweet ducks, bears, and sheep blankyclips! I'm thrilled!

But not for long. The new issue is that the factory has not yet released the bill of lading, which means that the shipping company cannot unload my goods and deliver them to me when then the ship arrives in Long Beach. Again, we are talking about a piece of paper. This time I email my Orthodox guys and plead with them to get Peter to speak with the factory. The shipping company has tried to reach the factory, but there's been no response. Interesting to note that I had no issues with the blanket factory when I asked them for this document.

Thank goodness for Peter, who makes sure the factory complies and gets the bill of lading turned in to the shipping company. My goods will be released and delivered. Un. Be. Lievable.

DOW JONES UNFRIENDS TARP

The Dow Jones Industrial Average responded to the news that the government decided to bail out the banks (the $700 billion!) with its worst week ever. First consumer confidence hit its lowest point *ever*, and then the Dow recorded its worst week *ever*. October 6 through October 10, 2008—down 22.1%. How much worse could this get?

There are so many issues that need to be addressed on the website that it's a wonder my head hasn't spun off. On the shipping page there's a random state that shows up if you're shipping to the same address as your billing address. Right now, there's no place to insert a discount code. How do I calculate shipping costs above eight gift sets if a store puts in a big order? Should there be a connection between my website and UPS? Can I get in my car and drive to Alaska right now?

The wholesaler page needs work, too. When a store buyer wants to put in an order, I'll be able to approve them and then they'll be able to purchase right from the site, but that requires the wholesale prices to be coded in the shopping cart. I'm waiting for Joe, the programmer, to get this done so we can finally go live with the site. We also need to add a Return Policy statement on the site. It feels very zen of me that I'm not just selling blankyclips but thinking of their possible return.

My web designer wants a list of twelve important "search engine words" that will help get my site listed higher up in a Google search. She will embed those words on my home page, and then if people are looking for something like my product but don't know the name blankyclip, it will come up in their search. How exciting to imagine someone searching for a clip for their blanket—like I did when that first blanket fell—and finding a blankyclip!

Li & Fung gives me a quote for blankyclips. They have found a factory that can make them for $1.68 per piece if I order 10,000 to 50,000 pieces. If I can't get my mold from the other factory, they can make a new mold for $1,800. I'll need to see some samples to find out if this new factory can make a quality product with quality plush.

Much more difficult to judge than plush is the right school to send Eli to for kindergarten. We've been told that the one near our duplex rental is terrible. There are homes in this neighborhood that are valued at north of a million dollars, and the local school sucks. Now I've got to tour schools and find out about magnet schools and lottery dates. To think that my parents could buy a lovely house with great public schools nearby and raise five kids on a single income is unreal. Such a fantasy now.

***

October 23, 2008. Yes, my parents had a house, but today I've got a website! We're going live with my brand spanking new website! There's more to upload in the press section, but we're good for now. The main thing is to launch it finally so people can see the product and put in orders. What a relief. A weight has been lifted from my shoulders.

I send out a huge email blast to let folks know about the website and to ask them to help spread the word. The response is amazing. Lots of stores are interested, and people are asking for wholesale info and letting me know how much they like the product. The photos are getting a great response too. There's been a flood of requests from mommy/baby blogs for free product in return for a mention of blankyclip on their site. Readers love giveaways, so I'm sending the blog writers the duck set with the ecru blanket to gift to their "winners." It should be a good way to get the word out.

When I get requests from stores in Canada, I tell them there might be a labeling issue with my product, but no one seems to know if this is true or not. I guess if they want to buy it and sell it as-is, then I can go ahead and ship to them. I'm also requesting seller's permits to be faxed to me for my records from all the wholesalers I've approved. To make sure I'm covered legally, my conservative accountant wants me to have copies of these from every store I sell to. There are just not enough hours in the day for me to get all this done on my own, but I do.

⁂

Today I learn that my main Orthodox guy is completely crazy.

He emails me an invoice, as he has paid the factory the balance on the order. Fair enough, but he's also paid BK $3,000 for his "quality control" work. Three grand for holding up a blankyclip every now and then and finding one or two that were not sewn correctly? "That's insane," I tell him. "If you'd told me that in advance, there's no way I would have approved. I cannot afford to pay him that."

Orthodox guy gets very angry with me, then says, "Okay, just pay half, but when the shipment arrives there is nothing you can say about any issues you might have with the order." Don't ask me why, but I agree to this. Even $1,500 seems ridiculously high, but it's not $3,000.

When I ask him to email me a new invoice with the adjusted total, he gets hysterical and says he doesn't know how to do that and his partner is out of the office and I should just send him the money I owe him. I explain patiently, "I have an accountant who has asked me to have invoices for everything I get charged for. I cannot pay only part of an invoice, as it will look like I have not paid correctly, so please send me a new invoice and I'll pay you immediately."

He screams at me some more, then calms down enough to say that he'll send a new invoice. "Great!" I say, and hang up feeling so icked-out by this man. What was the big problem? How is asking for a correct invoice cause for such anger? I won't be dealing with him again.

I meet with our pediatrician to show her the blankyclips and get a testimonial for my website. She connected me to my original bank loan officer, and now she's writing that she loves blankyclips because they're so useful and cute and safe, and that she'll be buying them as her favorite baby gift from now on. Her stamp of approval on my site can really help my business. She's been such an incredible support, with the Bank of America contact and now this. Now I get to say a doctor recommends the product!

I've been telling my podiatrist about my product, so when I come in for an appointment, I bring samples to show him. He flips out. He tells me that his wife's expecting twins and he wants to put in an order for two sets. He also wants brochures because he thinks he may know other people who will be interested in purchasing some. He could not be more supportive and doesn't seem at all fazed by the $48 price tag on the gift set.

Yay, a doctor still has money.

OCTOBER ENDS WITH SOME SCARY STATS

Get it? The end of October? Halloween? What could be scarier than the Dow Jones shrinking 27% in a single month? And unemployment boiling up to 6.5%? But, in the midst of all the bad economic news, one survey showed that Americans were still hopeful. Percentages increased on the number who planned to buy homes (prices were falling, maybe it was the right time), cars, and washing machines over the next six months.

November 3, 2008. My order of 10,000 (alright, 9,900) blankyclips from a small factory on a dirt road in Shenzhen is being delivered to my Public Storage unit. This time we're dealing with a real delivery company with two fit men and a real delivery truck. What's shocking this time are the boxes, which couldn't be more flimsy. Many are busted open with tape hanging off them, and blankyclips are strewn all over, black with dirt. A bank finally gives me a loan, and I fly to China twice to make sure that the product is manufactured correctly, and the factory ships my order this way? How did these rinky-dink boxes make it around the planet? Inside them are blankyclips in plastic bags so thin you can barely feel them. I'm incensed that after all this effort they would ship them this way. I've clearly lost a few hundred pieces through this negligence. And because of my agreement with the Orthodox guy that I can say nothing about any problems with the shipment, I can say nothing about the problems with the shipment. That was the deal.

Still, it's a relief that this incredibly hard phase of my business is over. Now I can get down to the task of selling blankyclips and growing my business. The next order I put in will most definitely be with another factory!

HOPE, IT WORKS

November 4, 2008. Barack Obama won the presidential election. There was a sense of renewed hope in 53% of American voters. This slim majority described themselves as either "excited" or "optimistic" about Obama serving as president. Maybe all that bailout money (that his predecessor approved) would end up working. Maybe the upcoming holiday season would infuse more consumer spending into the economy.

I'm feeling like the little engine that could as I head off to a Women's Night Out event in Hollywood to do a presentation about blankyclips. I love these monthly meetings. You get to hear about different businesses, and the gal who runs things is hilarious. I'm nervous because I'm one of the headliners of tonight's event, but I get lots of positive feedback for what I've accomplished so far and for the product. A man (wait, what?) in the audience wins a blankyclip gift set when I raffle one off. I hope he tells all his friends about his new favorite baby gift.

I have an order to ship out today to a gift shop in Ontario, Canada. My minimum order to wholesalers is two units of each design, but she wants four of each. Shipping is going to cost $65, but that's not an issue for her as she's used to paying high shipping fees from the U.S. How excited am I? I'm getting so much interest from Canadian stores that I've asked Joe to add Canada to the website so that people can order and ship there. My site is only set up for the U.S. since I never imagined I was going to ship anywhere else.

Today, I meet Ray, my friend and Palm Springs sales rep (who has yet to sell a single blankyclip in Palm Springs), at the LA Mart downtown. We're hoping to interest a showroom in carrying blankyclips. In addition to trade shows, the mart is a way for stores to find new products. I bring my seller's permit, business cards, brochures, sell sheets that explain what the product is, and of course sample blankyclip gift sets. We spend a couple of hours walking around, and it's pretty dead. No one is interested in us, and no one is looking at products in any of the showrooms. What about all that hopeful optimism on CNN just a week ago?

At long last I meet with the buyers for the Juvenile Shop. When I arrive for our scheduled appointment, one of them tells me that they aren't buying anything right now and tries to brush me off.

The other buyer says in that New York accent I so miss, "She's the gal who's been coming in to ask for our advice with her product. Remember those cute clips and the blankets?"

The first one warms up slightly. "Oh, yeah," she says, so we sit down in the back room and I take out my samples.

The nicer one says, "We'll take five and try them out," and then the meeting is over. I tell her that I actually have five units in my car and we can take care of it all right away, and she says fine, and within a matter of minutes I'm pocketing a check and driving away.

Since this meeting went so quickly, I have time to run over to The Grove's Pacific Theatre. Today is Mommy Movie day, which means a theater full of moms with their strollers and newborns. I have sixty blankyclips and brochures to give away. While they're watching the last few minutes of the movie, I manage to put duck, sheep, and bear blankyclips on the strollers parked in the theater lobby and use them to attach my brochure. The manager has given me permission to do so, as sometimes businesses do give out merchandise to the wonderful marketing opportunity known as new moms. I take a picture for my website and wait until the moms come out to the lobby. I'm nervous about how they'll react, but I'm putting myself out there anyway, because in 100 years . . . Most of the moms disappear quickly (so many full diapers to change), but the ones I'm able to introduce myself to seem very appreciative. The blankyclips are "really cute" and "such a great idea," and so we shall see if this little stunt pays off.

I learn that the U.S. Treasury is giving out $25 billion to Bank of America as part of the TARP program. I figure they must be doing all right now, so let me give them a call about lowering the interest rate on my line of credit. Pay it forward, BofA!

The gal at BofA tells me, "If you were to apply for a lower rate, it would require you to replace the current line of credit with another one at an increased interest rate." This is the exact opposite of what I'm asking for. "Plus, it would require you to show business tax returns for the past two years, and one year of personal." Since I have just started making money, there would be no history of cash flow in the business. I don't think she needs to continue, but she does. "Not only would your application most certainly be declined, but the balance of your current line of credit would go away too." Forget I ever called, lady!

My friend Cathy has a very successful jewelry business, and she agrees to meet with me to discuss how I can build my company. Her main advice is, "Get some blankyclips into the hands of celebrities. Then make sure they're photographed with your product and that these photos run in major magazines."

Oh, is that all? She suggests, "Contact the publicists of some pregnant celebrities, or celebrities who have just had babies, and offer to send them your product." Seems like a full-time job, chasing down celebrities, so I'm not sure how I'm going to squeeze this in. It would be nice to have a marketing division for my company, but that costs money I don't have.

Time to visit the Juvenile Shop to see how the blankyclips look in the store and find out if any have sold. Yes, one set sold. Yay! But the rest of them are stuck on a shelf near the crib bedding, and they're a mess. The blankyclips aren't secured to the ribbon the way I packaged them, and some of the blankets are unrolled. The whole thing is really depressing. I didn't anticipate customers taking the sets apart like this. How I sold them to the store is a completely different story from how they look now. I reroll the blankets and attach the blankyclips properly. I'm glad I stopped by, but I realize that five minutes after I leave another customer could just mess them up again. Apparently, this is what people do in stores. They take your blankets and unroll them, they take your blankyclips and unclip them from the ribbon, they take your product down until it's barely sellable.

HAPPY THANKSGIVING

November 20, 2008. The Dow Jones dropped to a six-year low. Almost everyone was afraid to ask how much worse this could get—especially the 6.8% of Americans who were unemployed. The holiday turned out to be a real turkey.

I look for some encouraging news, and I think I find it when I'm finally able to speak with Paige who owns a successful diaper pad company. It turns out to be not quite the call I'd hoped for, but it's a lesson for me. In the future, if someone asks me for advice about how to grow their business, it won't be helpful for me to tell them all about how successful I've been and how incredibly busy I am and how my sales have just grown tremendously, year after year, while I give them no advice at all. Even so, I offer to send her a sample, and she seems delighted by my generosity.

I sign up to be in a couple of holiday bazaars for some preschools. The deal is they get twenty percent of your sales, but it's a great way to keep spreading the word about blankyclip. And I finally send my notes to the rep from Li & Fung about the latest clip samples. They are not good, and I have to make sure to phrase my notes in a simple way. Can they even make the changes I want since the overall quality is so poor? How did I get such a great product from my first factory?

Did I say great product? I could never work with them again, but at least I did end up with a product I'm very proud of. But now what do I do? Assuming I can pay for a reorder, how will I find a good factory to work with?

I want to add some new options on the purchase page of my website so I can start selling the clips individually, but I'm having trouble uploading the photos because *it's always something.* At this point, I'm happy to sell individual clips, and I'm not the only one making concessions in order to attract business. Retail sales are the weakest they've been in thirty-five years, according to the *New York Times.* Lucky me. September and October were bad (massive understatement), and for companies like Target, Kohl's, and The Children's Place, November was worse. As November winds down, I look forward to the holiday shopping season, along with every other retailer, economist, and human being in America.

December 2008. We say, "Happy Holidays!" but some of us might be faking it a bit.

HO-HO-NO!

The U.S. hit a 26-year high for new unemployment claims in December, and 2008 will end up seeing two million U.S. jobs evaporate. December unemployment rose to 7.3%, and the National Bureau of Economics Research let everyone know that they existed (who knew?) by announcing that the recession had actually been underway since December 2007, so we should really be good at it by now.

Exciting news. My brother, who works as an online video producer, connects me with a producer of a nationally syndicated show called

Better TV, and she wants to do a segment about blankyclips! I send her samples and my press kit.

At my first holiday bazaar, I'm selling blankyclip gift sets at a discount and giving a percentage of my sales to the Jewish Community Center which is hosting the event for its preschool. It's the right demographic, for sure, so I'm happy to participate. My table is in an area pretty far from where the fun stuff for the kids is, like the games and the food. Very few people make it back here to the bazaar, and this is looking more and more like a waste of time. In the end, I sell about $150 worth of product, and I'm drained from sitting at a table for seven hours. The families come here to have a good time, which apparently means sticking to the games and food and not stopping by the bazaar for holiday gifts. Thankfully, my dear friend Bill takes over for the last hour and packs everything up, because I'm hosting a double birthday party for my kids who are turning two and five.

Yes, Eli is five now. Five years ago, I had the idea for blankyclip, and today I posted $150 in sales. That math doesn't feel right, but we party hard with a kids' music band and some great Persian food from a hole-in-the-wall downtown. Dagny is in a new dress from Hanna Andersson that was a total splurge, but she's only two once. It's her birthday, and I want her to look like a princess. And she does.

Looking around the party and seeing the kids so happy makes me feel so good. There is an abundance of food. The band is playing songs the kids love, and they're dancing and singing along. Eli is in heaven as the lead singer invites him to sing into the mic with her. Dagny finds a plastic toy to shake and stays right by my side with the biggest smile. It is a euphoric moment in time. I created this party for my kids because I love them, and I want their lives to be filled with joy. They don't know what it took for me to make it happen, nor do they need to know. I just want them to keep singing and dancing no matter what life hands them.

A great thing happens today. A friend sends a blankyclip gift set to his agent, and it turns out that the agent's wife, Emily, runs a high-profile blog/website that's all about getting the word out on great new baby items! It's called the Hot Moms Club. She wants to talk to me about my product. "I absolutely love it, and I haven't seen anything like it," she gushes to me on the phone. "I've seen a million products, and this one completely wowed me. I love how cute it is and that is has such a great purpose! I want to promote it on our site, and I want to gift it in some upcoming celebrity events I'm arranging."

Wow! This is just what Cathy said needed to happen. I offer to bring Emily some more product so she can use it in an upcoming shoot with TV host Victoria Recaño for *Fit Pregnancy* magazine. She also wants to give it to Brooke Mueller and Charlie Sheen for the baby shower she's putting together for the twins they're expecting. This is going to make a huge difference for my company. What luck that my friend happened to send her a blankyclip. He didn't even know that his agent's wife was involved in Hot Moms, he just knew they'd had a baby. I'm amazed that this woman is talking about promoting my business as if the fact that she has just given birth to her first child is not going to get in the way of her work.

I ship order #19 from my website. Without money to advertise, I have to be patient about building by word of mouth. I just need those mouths to start doing more talking.

I figure I should let Emily know that a couple of other celebrities now have blankyclips. Rebecca Romijn and Julianna Margulies were both given blankyclips by friends of theirs who are friends of mine. I'm not sure what she'll do with this information, but she's excited to hear the news. It's strange that there is validation from a celebrity having a product—if they own it, then it must be good. But that's how we operate, so I must play the game and try to get my product into their mystical hands.

Time for a much-needed break and a fun family trip. We're heading to Seattle to visit my husband's brother's family and—thanks to climate change—to show the kids some snow. As we sit waiting for our flight, I notice that my daughter is doing her same "I'm no longer a lefty" thing, which means she has nursemaid's elbow once again. We are in an airport about to take a flight. My husband looks at me and says, "You've watched it get fixed more than I have"—only once more— "so I think you're the one that's gotta do it."

I am not pleased with his logic, but he does have a point. The second time it happened, the pediatrician stressed the importance of getting the elbow fixed as quickly as possible, or there might be permanent damage. Time to tap into my inner goddess or warrior or something atavistic to help me do the impossible. I don't know where the courage comes from, but like those moms who can somehow lift a car, suddenly I am able to bend Dagny's arm and give it a sharp twist and put her elbow back where it belongs. The woman who is squeamish about all things medical and can barely put on a Band-Aid has come through for her daughter. A moment later the crying stops (hers, not mine) and she is pointing with her left hand at the "panes" she sees out the window. Shouldn't the mom who can do that be able to get her business off the ground?

New Year's Eve. I watch the ball drop on 2008, and I will it to get to the bottom of its descent—and the end of an arduous year—as quickly as it can.

2008 WAS THE YEAR OF THE RAT? THAT EXPLAINS IT

Economists, journalists, and homeowners noted that home prices dropped 40% this year. Just two months ago, the Conference Board announced that their Consumer Confidence Index had reached its lowest point ever, but records are made to be broken: U.S. consumers in December 2008 registered the *new* lowest confidence index in history. Experts suggested we all cross our fingers and hoped that flipping the page on our calendars would give the economy a psychological boost.

January 2009. Today Gary and I have a wonderful time drawing on all those years of working on short films while I pursued the acting/producing/director life. We're making a blankyclip infomercial! Times being what they are, we're using the best cheap labor around: our children. Gary writes a great script for Eli, who will be our spokesman. Dagny can say, "I got it!" now, so he writes around that new trick. We shoot it all in our little yard area, and the kids are excited about helping Mommy's company. We use our home video camera and keep it as simple as we can. My brother, the online video producer, is visiting from New York, so we make him the director of photography. Eli explains that his mom needed a way to keep his blanket from falling off his stroller and when she couldn't find anything safe and cuddly, she invented blankyclip. He's memorized his lines quickly, and he's wearing his fancy blazer, and he looks so cute I could eat him up. Dagny has a couple of things to say, and we've given her a few acting notes that she takes brilliantly. Gary tackles the job of editing it all together.

My plan is to put the video on the website, as another way of reaching people and getting the word out about blankyclip. It would be awesome if it went viral. I send out another big email blast to let everyone know about the video, and the response is great. People love it and find it hilarious and want to share it with their friends. My brother says, "It's the best infomercial I've ever seen," and he's not biased at all.

My giant email blast to everyone I ever knew about the launch of my website has produced a nice gesture. My friend Brooke who does PR wants to help me with some free work (she assumes correctly that I'm not in a position to hire a publicist), and I'm so flattered. She says the website looks awesome, and she loves the product and will do whatever she can do to support me. She does let me know that her focus is of course on her paying clients but that she'll add my name to pitches and try to get some interest from the magazines she works with.

WHY BOTHER SHIPPING IF NO ONE'S BUYING?
In 2008, because of the slowdown in consumer spending and business investment, global exports dropped for the United States (–18%), Japan (–27%), South Korea (–30%), and Taiwan (–42%).

People are clearly buying less which means I've got to work harder to get the word out. Brooke tells me that a local magazine called *L. A. Parent* is interested in possibly reviewing blankyclips. They need me to send them a sample. After seeing my website, they're really looking forward to checking them out. Just what I need! I can't believe how fast Brooke made this happen.

L. A. Parent gets the sample the next day, and an editor calls to say they're going to write a review. She loooooves (her o's) the product. The review will run in either their spring or summer *Expecting L. A.* issue. I remember reading reviews in those early mommy days and buying the items I read about, so this is fabulous news. All I can think about these days is how to get people to buy this darn product with my non-existent marketing budget.

I hit some upscale boutiques in West Hollywood. One isn't the right fit, as they do custom bedding for cribs and design baby rooms. But the other, Bel Bambini, is filled with everything from strollers and baby gear to toys to bath stuff, clothing, and gifts. I ask for the name of the buyer and am told how to contact her. I definitely want to get in here.

January 15, 2009. Life changes in an instant. My husband is laid off.

"The bank took away the company's line of credit. The orders have shrunk, and since I was the last guy brought on, I'm the first one out. There's nothing I can do," he tells me. He seems to be in shock.

I am immediately in freakout mode. This is so scary. We have no savings or safety net. The news is all about people getting laid off and how unemployment keeps going up and up, but I did not think this would happen to us. There are so many people looking for work. How is Gary going to find a job? I know crying doesn't help, but I cannot stop the tears.

The next night I take the kids to see *Annie* at the Kodak Theatre and am again in tears when they sing the "Thank You, Herbert Hoover" song about being unemployed. The theater is dark, and the moms I'm with don't seem to notice, thank goodness. I'm too embarrassed to tell them that my husband is no longer employed. These women have enviable household incomes and live in beautiful houses that they own. We're sitting in the same row, but I feel a million miles away from them. It certainly does not feel like the sun will come out tomorrow.

I must keep moving forward, so I bring my samples to the Right Start. They have stores everywhere, and I'd really like to get in there. I show my samples to an employee, and she really likes them. She suggests I contact the buyer and gives me her info. A ray of hope.

I'm back at Bel Bambini to meet with Kristina, the buyer. She likes the product and decides to buy fifteen individual clips. She sells high-end blankets, so she doesn't want to carry my blanket, but she'd like to try out the clips. I happen to have fifteen all ready to go in my car, so I'm able to sell and deliver all at once and save her the shipping costs. She doesn't have much time for chit-chat (buyer protocol), so after she writes the check, she abruptly goes back to her office. But I'm in Bel Bambini, people!

Emily sends me the article that will appear in *Fit Pregnancy's* March issue with Victoria Recaño. The picture of the pink blanket and white blankyclip on her stroller is completely washed out, but they've listed my website, and I think that's what counts. A national magazine! This could help get the ball rolling at last.

Gary applies for yet another job on Monster or CareerBuilder or LinkedIn, I can't remember which. The job's in another part of the country, and there's no relocation offered. Before I can get too upset about the idea of moving, he points out that hundreds of others have also applied for the job. And this time, like all the other times, he never hears back. When I ask him what we are going to do, he doesn't have an answer for me. That voice in my head that wants me to worry about everything is having a very good time right now. We have two kids, and we rely on his income. There is a lot to worry about.

JUST STOP, PLEASE

My husband and 599,999 more Americans lost their jobs in January 2009, which helped unemployment reach 7.8%. The outlook was bleak. And apparently ubiquity offered no protection, as Starbucks announced that 6,700 baristas would join the unemployed and that after closing 600 stores in 2008, they would close another 300.

I feel like I'm in a race against . . . everything and nothing tangible at all. The ground is collapsing under my feet, but I keep running as fast as I can. As the calendar closes on the month, I ship order #32 from my website.

February 2009. I'm not sure why, but I'm still going back and forth with the latest Chinese factory about the samples. I don't have the money to manufacture more clips, and the owner wants to know when I'm putting an order in. The samples squeak and are full of problems, so I can focus on that and not on putting in my order.

I find a great contact on the list of folks who attended the Vegas trade show: Angela, the buyer for Buy Buy Baby. I call her, and she tells me to send her some samples. This is fabulous. They're a huge chain! She emails me as soon as she receives the samples saying that "the items are great," but she has a few issues to discuss with me. Would I please call her? Oh yes, I will, woman!

Finally, I get Angela on the phone.

"I love the samples!" she tells me. "Everyone in my office loves your product!" But her problem, or my problem, is that they can only sell items that are packaged in a poly or vinyl bag with an insert card. They need to hang on a peg and be covered to keep them clean. She would love to test blankyclip in a couple of stores and online, but it needs to be peggable. Both the clips and the blanket need to be in the bag. Maybe zippered like JJ Cole does. She would want twelve of each design for three stores, so that's thirty-six per store, and twelve of each for online. A total of 144 units.

"Solve the packaging, and then we'll talk again," she says, and vanishes. Okay, hangs up, but the moment feels pretty out of this world.

I send her a follow-up email and mention that talking to her makes me miss New York. (Oh, that accent!) She tells me that if I come to visit, she'll buy me a hotdog. I dare not let her know that I do not eat meat (pescatarian since 1986!), because we now have a nice rapport going. Gary asks if I would eat a street hotdog to get into Buy Buy Baby. I ate steak when I shot a Quincy's Steakhouse commercial years ago, so it wouldn't be the first time I sold myself out. Pass the mustard.

Since there's no Buy Buy Baby store near me, I head to Babies "R" Us to research clear bags and see how other companies package their products. I send out emails asking for referrals for packaging designers.

I need to get this figured out quickly, as I don't want Angela to lose interest. Turns out there are tons of people in the business of packaging design, but I cannot afford any of them. I'm paying plenty of bills as it is. Not to brag, but I seem to be better at this than my own state of California.

THE GOLDEN STATE

February 3, 2009. The government of California, in day 89 of a budget stalemate, *ran out of money*. It issued IOUs on all bills whose payment wasn't mandated by law. Just like the rest of us would have done, except California didn't get sued or go to jail. It did, however, lay off 20,000 state employees, and lucky for us, state tax refunds didn't get sent out.

The magazine that did the article with Victoria Recaño is *Pregnancy* magazine, not *Fit Pregnancy* magazine. I had that wrong. Emily of the Hot Moms Club says, "*Fit Pregnancy* will be covering the baby shower we gave Victoria, so blankyclip may be in that as well. *Life & Style* magazine definitely covered her shower, so you can use that as press too, since blankyclips were part of the shower. That issue is on newsstands now." I can't get over the press that this one woman has generated for my company. Thank you, Emily. Off to the newsstand I go!

TOYS WERE US

In February 2009, and after eighty-seven years of operation, KB Toys closed the last of its 605 stores. Then Babystyle, a national baby retailer, was sold to the Right Start and went out of business, likely because Right Start filed for bankruptcy and closed its thirty stores. Also in February, Los Angeles baby boutique Spirituali shut down for good.

Okay, while there may be fewer and fewer places to sell blankyclips, I feel like I'm making progress. I've got interest from a national chain. I'm getting some nice (and free) press. My website is humming along. But all around me are signs to keep running as fast as I can.

FEB 2009 CCI SAYS "TAKE THAT!" TO JAN 2009 CCI

February 2009 left all the old Consumer Confidence Index records in the dust. The headline could've been copied and pasted from October, December, and January: CONSUMER CONFIDENCE AT AN ALL-TIME LOW. Unemployment rose to 8.3%. Stop me if you've heard this before, but the number of Americans filing first-time unemployment claims was the highest in 27 years. Speaking of which, Panasonic announced plans to close 27 manufacturing facilities. And if you thought the electronics industry had it tough, be glad you weren't in the auto industry (unless you are, or more likely *were*, in the auto industry). Nissan cut 20,000 jobs. General Motors cut 10,000 jobs. Even BMW and Bentley sent 850 and 220 people, respectively, to the unemployment line. Saab filed for bankruptcy. And GM and Chrysler went to the U.S. government and said, "If you want to keep seeing crackerjack results like that, we're going to need an additional $21.6 billion from you."

Dagny is delighted that the whole family can be at her toddler music class today, not that I recommend unemployment as a means to squeeze in family time on a Monday morning. We sing in Spanish about *los elefantes* while we ignore the biggest elephant: hubby needs a *trabajo*.

March 2009. I meet with my publicist friend Brooke to discuss what other magazines she wants to target. She works out of her gorgeous home and has a nanny watching her son. I'm so impressed by the business she's built. She has an employee who shows me how to create a nice display with the magazine cover and the magazine article where blankyclip is mentioned, all on one page. I wish I had people who could do things like this for me.

I scour Craigslist for packaging designers, and it's crazy what I hear from them. The latest quote is for $7,500. Do they not realize they're on Craigslist? Not where I would be looking if I had that kind of money.

Approaching packaging design from a cost perspective, I discover a company called Imex that makes stock clear vinyl bags that can hang from their rope handles. They've sent me samples that look good, though they're a tad too small. I figure out a way to squeeze a blanket and two blankyclips in the bag. Now I just need a cardboard insert with all the info printed on it. The Imex sales gal is easy to work with and gives me a good rate on the bags. The orders that Buy Buy Baby will place are contingent on Angela liking my packaging, so I better be right about this choice.

I'm so focused on getting the packaging ready for Buy Buy Baby that I'm stunned when I receive a Notice of Abandonment from the U.S. Patent and Trademark Office. I've not submitted my Statement of Use, and I have no extensions left, so now the USPTO is telling me that I no longer have the trademark. After all these years, I have to start all over again. I file once more, to the tune of $275. I have my GoDaddy-purchased domain name up and running. I have a business email address. I'm actually selling blankyclips and using the mark now, so "pending use" is no longer an issue. That should help.

Gary used to work at Stila Cosmetics and still has contacts there. I'm going to work with Julio, a Stila packaging designer, on the cardboard insert for my polybag. The insert has to be small enough that you can see the blankyclips inside the bag, but big enough that you can read the product information on the card. We are creating one card that can be used for all three designs to save on printing costs. Julio has an eye for what the consumer needs to see on a package, and I feel I'm in good hands.

I commit to be in a trade show called Baby Celebration that is open to the public, which means I can sell product directly to consumers. My friend Heather, who has a maternity clothing line, is going as well. She suggests that I drop my price for the show and try to make as many sales as possible. She also tells me she hopes that the economy doesn't discourage people from coming to the show and buying. Why does it make me feel better to hear that she's struggling with sales too?

I meet with Julio to give him a sample vinyl bag and to discuss ideas about what the card should look like. I give him a disc with photos and copy I'd like him to consider for the packaging. Julio loves what I've written and praises the great quality of the photos. He's so encouraging about my product. These are the moments I wish I could bottle, the creative state of possibility.

ARE YOU LYING DOWN?
WELL, THE STOCK MARKET IS

March 6, 2009. The Dow Jones dropped to 6,626 points. A year and a half ago, it was over 14,000 points. 663,000 more Americans joined the ranks of the unemployed, and the unemployment rate found its way to 8.7%.

Should I tell my friends how depressed we are about Gary being out of work? Of all the fields for him to be looking for a job, manufacturing, whether of golf clubs or cosmetics, seems like the absolute worst. I am building a business, and I want people to see how optimistic I feel about it despite details like we have no income at the moment.

Thank you, thank you, universe! At last, a sign that things might work out. *L. A. Parent's Expecting* magazine makes blankyclip their top pick in their Spring 2009 issue, Oh, yes they do! Check out what appears on March 18, 2009:

> Baby secured in stroller? Check. Baby covered with blanket? Check. Ready to roll. But then the blanket falls off into the dirty street! Unless you happen to have blankyclips ($48 for two clips and plush blanket, www.blankyclip.com).
>
> Designed by a local mom, these loose-tension clips will hold a blanket fast to any model stroller, car seat or carrier but won't pinch little fingers. They're also a sheep,

a duck or a bear (your choice)! True security at last. Available locally at Bel Bambini in West Hollywood and Juvenile Shop in Sherman Oaks.

What a fantastic plug! It should really help drive sales.

The vinyl polybags arrive. Yay! They're not what I ordered. Boo! The color on the trim is slightly different from the sample. I have to send them back and wait for another shipment while Angela at Buy Buy Baby waits for me to get it all together.

I take a photo showing how the vinyl package looks with the cardboard insert we've been working on and send it to Angela. She's a woman of few words and just responds with "like!!!!!" (exclamation points, hers). Me too. Now to get those inserts printed.

March 24, 2009. Holy moly. Shortly after I meet with Julio to discuss printing the insert card, he finds out that all the employees at Stila have been furloughed. They won't be getting paid, yet are technically still employed. Julio still wants to work with me on the blankyclip packaging, but his life has been turned upside down. I feel so bad for him. I can't help thinking that if Gary had stayed with Stila, he'd be without income anyway and still going to work. Insane.

AND THE HITS JUST KEEP ON COMING . . .
March 2009. Goody's Family Clothing closed the last of its 500 stores. Whitehall Jewelers shut down its 373 stores. Fortunoff went out of business. Zales shuttered 115 of its stores. Ritz Camera Centers filed for bankruptcy.

The woman who runs a little boutique in a Florida hotel and who wanted to carry blankyclips there now says that because her sales were basically nil and she "had no season" this year, she can't buy more product at the moment. She's stopped all buying. If the stores aren't buying product to sell, how the heck am I going to get my product sold?

EXPERTS CONFIRM: SKY, BLUE / GRASS, GREEN

April 16, 2009. The U.S. Federal Reserve confirmed that consumers have been pulling back on purchases and that businesses have been canceling planned investments and laying off workers. Additionally, financial institutions have been shrinking their assets (i.e., not taking investment risks) to improve their chances of making it through the recession. This has been referred to as the "paradox of deleveraging"—i.e., strategies that may work for individuals or firms but magnify the distress of the recession as a whole.

I do the pared-down set up for the Baby Celebration trade show. The show is pretty fun, though it seems like cost is still an issue. People are being really careful with their dollars, but I do get some sales. A highlight for me is when a toddler is holding a duck blankyclip (okay, so maybe I gave it to her) and then she doesn't want to let it go when her mom wants to move on, so Mama buys it. You do what you gotta do.

APRIL SHOWERS BRING MAY FLOWERS

Or they just get everything wet. General Motors revealed plans to close thirteen factories in the U.S. and Mexico. Yahoo! announced cuts of 600–700 jobs (is not even the internet safe?). And the April unemployment rate rose to 9.0%.

My associates Dagny and Eli come with me to Michaels craft store, to buy some materials so I can try to repair blankyclips that arrived with deformities. I hope to find padding for the ones that don't have enough in the clip area. I need thread to match the fabric for the ones with holes along the seams. Maybe I can save the clips that arrived with problems, as I need to sell as much as I can from this order. God knows how I'll get enough money to put in a reorder and keep running my business.

May 2009. It's Mother's Day and also my birthday, so I am awoken by the most eager of breakfast makers. The kids present me with the cards they've drawn and a plate of sliced fruit they've arranged to form a smiley face. Did ever a queen dine as well? I think not.

I'm working on a mailing to the 2,500 stores that I have info for from the Vegas trade show. Patty has designed a wonderful postcard, and I get it made by Vistaprint online. Every penny I spend for advertising and marketing is a stretch for me, but I have to do it.

A friend suggests that I take some blankyclips to a boutique in nearby Glendale. This is a very good suggestion because the owner/buyer loves them and buys $117 worth of product. I love that it's a store close by, and I can now let people know they can shop for my product there. If only it were this easy to get in all the boutiques.

Fixing the faulty blankyclips isn't as easy as I'd hoped. Turns out I'm not a seamstress. I drive to Michael Levine's, the fab fabric store downtown, to see if I can find one. They don't offer that service and don't seem to know anyone who can help me.

At long last, I have 1,000 printed blankyclip logo stickers and 2,500 cardboard inserts, and I'm finally able to ship three packaged samples to Angela at Buy Buy Baby. On February third, 2009, she asked me to send her a sample after I emailed her about my product. It's May eighth, 2009, and I've gone from not having mass packaging to having mass packaging, and it all happened in this country. Miraculous. I'm celebrating with some pizza for dinner because it just feels like a party when pizza is in the house. And I deserve a party.

***

May 21, 2009. Great news today! Angela at Buy Buy Baby loves the new packaging. What she doesn't love is the price, but I can't do too much about it. I've already dropped the gift set price from $48 to $39.99 for her stores. She thinks it would sell better at $24.99, but that would mean lowering my wholesale price to $12.50, and there's no way I can afford that. Plus, I have to consider keeping close to my prices for boutiques and my website. I need the $20 wholesale price badly. There's not going to be any profit for me at this point, but the plan is to create a demand and somehow be able to put in a reorder. Getting into Buy Buy Baby is a huge coup and a step in that direction.

It's becoming a part-time job just figuring out all the steps involved in the Bed Bath & Beyond (owners of Buy Buy Baby) vendor application. I need an EDI company that will process the orders Buy Buy Baby sends me. It's an electronic system that's standard for these big stores. Yet another expense for me. Yippee!

There's not much negotiating when you become a vendor at Bed Bath & Beyond. I fill out a twelve-page vendor application that makes my head spin. I'm going to need to add them to my insurance policy. I find out that their payment terms are Net 60, (they'll pay in sixty days) except when you ship to a new store and then it's Net 90 (they'll pay in ninety). Are you kidding me? And they get a twenty percent discount for a new store on top of that! I have to ship my product by SKU, one color per box. Angela will send me orders from the stores, and I'll be getting separate orders from their website folks. My head spins some more . . .

I get into another boutique store today, the Butter Paddle in Los Gatos. It's a gift store, and they learned about my product from my postcard mailing. Then I'm contacted by a baby store that's strictly on the internet, and I can't see how that's a good idea for me at this moment in time. I don't want people to buy from their website instead of mine. I'll only get the wholesale price if I sell to them. Better to get full price on my own site. With Buy Buy Baby, it's a different situation because they're a huge chain and are also selling in their stores. I think I need to stick to stores that may do both but are not just online.

HOW TO SURVIVE ON $161 MILLION A DAY

TARP announced that JPMorgan Chase and American Express won't require any more bailout money! It turned out that the $25 billion and $3.4 billion they received over the past six months was enough. Automakers weren't quite as savvy as these financial giants. Chrysler planned to terminate 789 dealerships in the U.S., while GM planned to terminate 1,100 of them. GM kept the hits coming by announcing a $6 billion loss in the first quarter of 2009. And the May 2009 unemployment rate increased to 9.4%.

My friend from the Vegas show with the lunch bag and backpack company has given me a name to contact. He's part-owner of a factory in China, but he's American and lives in northern California. My friend didn't end up working with him because of her product needs, but she had a good feeling about him. She thinks I might have success with him on my product.

What a difference it is to talk to a sane guy in manufacturing! He's taken a look at my website and wants me to send him samples, both to his office in the U.S. and to the factory in China. I'm not ready to put in a production order just yet, but the whole process of getting samples made takes so long that I'm glad to be starting it off with a new factory.

<hr>

June 2009. USPTO responds to the new trademark application I filed in March. They tell me my entity is "indefinite." My application indicates an individual person's name (mine) in the trademark owner's entity space, but a corporation was set up as the owner. "If applicant is an individual, applicant should request that the entity be amended to 'individual' and must indicate his/her country of citizenship for the record."

Also, my "specimen is unacceptable." They're not talking about a specimen like the one Gary had to leave when we were having fertility issues. They're talking about a photo of my packaging ribbon with the trademark R in a circle above the name, and it's unacceptable because "it does not show the applied for mark used in connection with any of the goods specified in the application." I was supposed to show the ribbon as it's used in my packaging. The photo I sent them is a close-up of the logo on the ribbon.

And that's not all they are unhappy with me about. The application was filed for "baby strollers." However, "the specimens show use of the mark for accessories used with baby strollers, and not the baby strollers themselves. Specifically, the mark is shown on clip-like items. That is not the same thing as baby strollers."

Oops. But it does seem a bit severe to respond with, "The undersigned being warned that willful false statements and the like are punishable by fine or imprisonment, or both."

Again with the imprisonment. Must I always be heading to prison? I'm just trying to sell a stroller accessory, people.

I give up on trying to do the trademark application on my own and ask my patent attorney to file for me. Henry files two applications, one for the word blankyclip and the other for my logo. You win, USPTO. You want applications done by attorneys, and now you'll have two. I spent too many years and too many dollars trying to do it on my own. Enough.

LUCK OF THE IRISH

June 2009. Economists predicted that Ireland, with its 11.8% unemployment rate, might not recover from the recession until 2014. The United States lagged behind Ireland with a paltry 9.5% unemployment rate. Qantas Airways canceled $3.1 billion worth of orders with Boeing. GM and retailer Eddie Bauer filed for bankruptcy.

June 22, 2009. My first order from Buy Buy Baby comes in for three stores: one in Paramus, New Jersey, one in Garden City, New

York, and—most exciting for me—one in the Chelsea neighborhood of New York City. Each store orders thirty-six units, twelve of each design, for a total order of 108 units. If all goes well in these three stores, they will roll me out to the others. These three are their testing ground for my product. Nerve-wracking, to say the least, but it feels like I'm finally on my way. The economy is in free-fall and my husband is still very much unemployed, but I can feel my running feet squelch out of the quicksand.

9

The Fun Just Doesn't Stop

ECONOMISTS CRUSH THE RECESSION!
The National Bureau of Economic Research announced that the Great
Recession ended when June 2009 came to a close. Yay!

With the Great Recession behind us, I spend every waking moment
packing up 108 blankyclip gift sets in the vinyl bags for the Buy
Buy Baby order.

Packaging the order involves the following steps:

1) cut blankyclip ribbon strips

2) take blanket out of shipping plastic

3) shake blanket so fuzzy fleece bits fall off

4) fold and roll blanket tightly, then have hubby hold blanket
   down while I tie the ribbon around it tightly to ensure it
   will fit into the vinyl bag

5) inspect each blankyclip carefully and remove any dirt or
   black threads

6) make sure sheep, duck, and bear arms and legs hang correctly

7) check sheep, duck, and bear padded areas

8) spruce up duck's white hair, bear's ears, and sheep's ears

9) place barcode sticker on cardboard insert

10) remove useless piece of paper that comes inside every vinyl bag

11) inspect vinyl bag for loose threads or issues with rope handles

12) put blankyclip logo sticker on top of vinyl bag

13) push cardboard insert into vinyl bag

14) ~~cram~~ insert blanket with two blankyclips on either side, adjusting sheep, duck, and bear arms and legs and heads so blankyclips present nicely in the bag, and finally,

15) put plastic hang tag piece through zipper and bag so that zipper can't be opened at the store unless unit has been bought.

One down, 107 to go.

As excited as I am about the Buy Buy Baby order, I know I need to keep getting the word out. This is why I shoot a little video about blankyclip with a blogger. We meet in Griffith Park, and she interviews me about my invention, how I came up with it, and how I got it made. It's a subject I enjoy talking about. I bring a stroller, a blanket, and some blankyclips, feeling like a happenin' mom inventor. We shoot it all on her little Flip camera that sits on a tripod. Amazing that this is all it takes these days to have a video on the web.

Then I'm back to packing up the gift sets. Our home looks like a factory, so I'm beyond ecstatic when FedEx picks up my nine boxes with 108 vinyl-packaged blankyclips and ships them to the three Buy Buy Baby stores. Wonder of wonders, they'll be hanging on pegs in these huge stores in a few days.

I send a blankyclip gift set to the winner of yet another blog contest. It's the bajillionth one I've sent out to different blogs, and it's getting a little annoying. The blogs don't seem to lead to sales, just to moms trying to win free product. Maybe it's good for getting the word out, but it doesn't seem to be moving the needle. It certainly makes the winners happy, and I'm at least getting good reviews, but no one is buying on my site. Come on, people, didn't you hear? The great recession ended this month!

Today I call the three Buy Buy Baby stores to introduce myself to the managers and let them know I'm sending them an additional bear blankyclip that I've attached to a chain so it can be used as a demo. "Since the packaged products are sealed and no one can open them, having a sample that customers can touch will be really helpful," I explain. "It's a new product, and there's never been a baby-friendly clip out there before. I want people to feel the loose tension and the padding and see how easy they are to open." The managers all seem supportive.

The good folks at Buy Buy Baby are selling my product on their website, which is great. What's not so great is that they charge $200 per item sold on their site, so that's $600 for the three gift sets. They want me to write the copy that'll appear with the product and send them high-rez photos. Also, they want samples of the product, so I need to send them three packaged sets. And even though I sell on my own website (and don't charge myself $600), I clearly don't get the traffic they do, so I tell myself it's a great opportunity. I pay the $600, and the web order comes in for thirty-six sets.

CONSUMER CONFIDENCE, WEARY OF THE CLIMB, SLIDES DOWN AGAIN

After a series of record lows, the Consumer Confidence Index had been creeping upward from March until May. But that exhausting climb proved to be too much for the anemic CCI, and it reacted by stumbling down again in June. When asked to comment on why it didn't seem to be able to get any upward momentum, CCI responded, "Have you seen the unemployment rate? It's up to 9.5%. How confident would *you* be if almost one out of ten of you were out of a job?"

July 2009. I'm off to New York City to meet with the three Buy Buy Baby store managers and set up a display to promote blankyclips in their stores. All the managers think it's a good idea. I want to educate the employees, make myself known and thought about in their stores, and get some buzz going about the product. I have samples with me but will basically use their strollers and try to demo blankyclip to as many customers as I can. My family in New York is astonished that I'm traveling back east without my kids (Gary is home with them), but there's no way I could handle them on top of what I'll be doing. This is a business trip, and those don't tend to include toddlers.

First, I go to the Chelsea store on Seventh Avenue in Manhattan. It's crazy busy and has two floors, and I have no idea where my product is. I ask an employee where the stroller accessories are, and she points me downstairs. I decide to find my product before approaching a manager. Imagine my surprise when I finally find some bear blankyclip sets but no ducks and no sheep. Really? They have only one design out? How exactly am I supposed to get my product bought if it isn't even out and available? I calmly approach a manager, and he tells me that he'll be with me in a minute, which turns into fifteen before he's able to speak with me. I let him know who I am and why I'm here and that I'd like the other two designs brought out.

This leads to a massive hunt for duck and sheep blankyclips. Lots of walkie-talkies and guys from the loading dock, and no one knows where they are, and I'm borderline hysterical. I've flown 3,000 miles to introduce myself to the store and to the public, and I've received a confirmation from FedEx that all the boxes arrived, and now no one knows where the heck they are?

I end up in the loading dock, where the boxes are signed for. It's so busy here that no one seems to mind me poking around, but I find no trace of my blankyclip boxes. Back in the store, one of the managers takes pity on me and leaves the floor and all the customer chaos to help me. And miracle of miracles, he finds my boxes. Someone thought they were more bear clips, so they got buried. If I hadn't physically come to this store, I wouldn't have known that the sheep and duck blankyclips weren't even out on the floor. I'm beside myself, but I try my best to be as smiley as possible and win these managers over.

I set my display up with one of the store's strollers and my blankyclip samples. I introduce myself to as many managers as possible. They're young and have no idea about my product. Now that the other two designs are out, it's exciting to see the vinyl bags hanging on their pegs, looking very legit and worthy of being bought. I call on my performer background and just start talking to whomever I can. New Yorkers are usually in a rush and don't want to be scammed, so I have to sound authentic and confident.

The store's packed with thousands of items. If customers are going to notice my product and understand my product and then buy my product, it's crucial to have the employees help promote it. When I tell them that I'm the mom who invented the product and show them baby Dagny on the brochure, it seems to get them excited. I explain a blankyclip's purpose and encourage them to mention to a customer who buys a stroller that there's a product out there that will keep a blanket from falling off that new stroller.

I see a pregnant woman with her nose buried in a copy of *Baby Bargains,* and hear her ask an employee how to find a product mentioned in the book. It occurs to me that I have to get blankyclip in that book. I was that same pregnant woman years ago, and *Baby Bargains* was my absolute how-to guide because how else would I know which stroller or car seat I should buy? Since blankyclips aren't mentioned in her book, the woman barely gives me a second glance. But the performer in me comes out, again, and I'm enjoying the spectacle. I see a harried dad with twin newborns and make sure that he leaves with two sets in the five minutes he's in the store. I'm not sure if I'm the ringleader or the clown in this circus, but fortunately I have no shame when it comes to making as big an impression as I can in a short time.

I can see how busy the employees are with the customers and how little time they're going to have to think about my product. They have to deal with all the millions of questions that new parents have, and there's all that gear, and no one knows much about any of it. My blankyclips are in the stroller accessories section, and it's not an area you'd notice unless you were really looking for an accessory. I ask a manager about possibly moving some blankyclips to a more visible area. I explain that my product makes a great baby shower gift, and he says the gift section is upstairs and he can't move me into a different section. He's a manager for stroller accessories only. I'm glad I'm here to see all the elements that go into selling in a large store. Getting blankyclip in the store is one thing, but getting it out in a customer's shopping cart is another.

Next day, I'm off to Garden City, Long Island, to hit that store and meet Angela, the woman who's changed the future of my business. Angel Angela. My blankyclips have better placement in this store and are also available near the register. Two points of purchase? Very cool. I introduce myself to the managers on the floor, and they direct me to Angela's office at the back of the store where the corporate offices are.

Angela is a surprisingly petite woman. I was expecting someone larger than life, as she has taken on mythic proportions for me. She shows me to a conference room, and we sit down to talk about blankyclip in her stores. She tells me that it's all about sales and she'll be tracking how well it does and we shall see. It's not the warmest of meetings, but she's a buyer and I'm a client and it's just about business. I learn that Buy Buy Baby is run by the son of the owner of Bed Bath & Beyond and that Angela has numbers to hit, and it's a stressful time for the company, as for all companies. If a product doesn't do well, she has to replace it with one that does. I'm so intimidated by people like her. I manage to get myself in the room only to find myself doubting I should be there.

As I peruse the floor of the Garden City store, I begin to strategize. Placement isn't an issue here, so my goal is to meet the managers and make sure they understand the product. Let them know that I'm a mom inventor with a small (extremely small) business. Hey, that's my daughter on the cardboard insert! I so appreciate their support, etc. Also, I need to make sure that the sample I sent them is hanging correctly near my display. I try to be friendly and not too pushy.

The last store on my East Coast tour means a bus ride from Port Authority out to Paramus, New Jersey. Fortunately, my aunt who lives in the area, can pick me up and take me to the store. I find a manager, and he isn't sure if my product is out on the floor yet. He's running around looking for it when I stumble upon my vinyl bags hanging from a large pole stuck in a floor stand. It's not great placement, but he tells me that he can move me to a better spot—exactly why this trip is so important. With me there, he has a reason to find the best place in the store for my product. I really need the help of these store managers to direct their customers to blankyclips.

Back in NYC, I do my pitch at Albee's, a great store on the Upper West Side. They love blankyclips! The store's packed to the gills with other products, though, so they only want to try six units to see how they sell. Right now, I need exposure, so having them in Albee's could help my Buy Buy Baby sales. When I see a product in different stores, it seems much more credible than if I only see it in one.

I return to the Chelsea store, and already things are a mess. They've changed the placement of the blankyclip bags which are now hanging so low that some touch the floor. The bags have been handled by customers and put back on the peg backwards. There's one with a broken rope handle. It looks awful. All this can happen in just a few days? I organize them, sort them by design, and make the display area look as appealing as I can—but I won't be here every few days to do this.

On the mean streets of Manhattan, I have fun giving out blankyclips to parents pushing strollers. One mom has the awful black binder clip holding her blanket to her $1,200 stroller, and she's delighted to have a cute duck blankyclip instead. I also give out brochures and never fail to mention that blankyclips are available at Buy Buy Baby. Credibility.

My East Coast blankyclip tour is at an end. I return to LA, and my husband is still unemployed. We've gone from always giving each other a kiss before bed to skipping it sometimes. We aren't fighting, but we aren't together the way we used to be. As our debt increases each month, an invisible layer of resentment is starting to build.

I call the manager at Albee's to follow up. He told me he'd be placing an order for six bagged gift sets, but I haven't received it. Am I really spending my time leaving messages for someone to put in an order for six gift sets? Why did he say he would if he wouldn't?

As I begin the downward tailspin I go into when people do not keep their word, I get an email from a cousin who recently found me on the internet. We are connected through our great-grandparents who were siblings in Poland. This long-lost cousin sends me a document he tracked down that shows the members of my grandfather's family who were killed by the Nazis. My grandfather submitted these Pages of Testimony to Yad Vashem, the World Holocaust Remembrance Center, and I am seeing them all in an email.

I read the names of my relatives who were killed. A minute before, I was bummed that I didn't get an order for six blankyclip gift sets.

The world keeps spinning, and now I am kvelling. blankyclip is in this month's *Fit Pregnancy* magazine. The Victoria Recaño baby shower got half a page, with a mention of blankyclips as one of her favorite gifts. I'm so grateful to Emily for making this happen. Then I hear from a high school friend on the East Coast who saw *Fit Pregnancy* in her doctor's waiting room and loved the blankyclip mention. I'm astounded by what being in a national publication does for my exposure, not to mention my self-esteem. After the teeniest bit of harassing, that Florida store, Baby Love, puts in an order. I also get an order from a Bed Bath & Beyond in Stamford, Connecticut, which confuses me, so I call them. It's a new thing they're doing, putting a baby section in large Bed Bath & Beyond stores in towns without a Buy Buy Baby. Good news.

August 2009. I'm at the Pump Station in Santa Monica with a basket of single blankyclips, three gift sets with the blankets, the *Fit Pregnancy* article that mentions blankyclips, some brochures, and an order form. I really want to get into this store. A manager tells me that I should come back the next day to talk to Eric. He makes all the buying decisions.

The next day, Eric says he likes my product but is only interested in the single clips. He sells too many high-end blankets already. He thinks $15 per clip is too expensive and wants me to drop my price to $12.95. And he doesn't give half for wholesale price; he likes to do a 55/45 split. *And* he wants me to guarantee sales. Really? I can't see how I can agree to these terms. He asks me to leave the basket with twelve single blankyclips so that he can show them to his partner as she makes all the decisions. Jeez. I leave the basket, but I don't have a good feeling about any of this. I'm becoming less interested in this store by the second. Too much attitude.

Since I never do get that order from Albee's, I decide to ship the six vinyl bags to my friend Randy and have him hand-deliver the order—along with an invoice. It's a bit ballsy, but I'm going to go for it (well, I'm making Randy go for it). I know they want the six units because they told me so when I was in New York, so I'm just helping them out since they're so busy. Right?

Randy is slightly mortified about being the messenger, but he's willing to bring the box to them. He reports back that they were friendly and surprised and didn't seem offended at all. Did I just get myself an order? It's kind of like showing up at an audition without an appointment. It can piss people off or they can be impressed by your gutsy gesture.

What would I do without my friends? When Elizabeth, one of my oldest friends, comes over, I tell her I'm not all that upset that Gary is still unemployed, it's just that I can't look at him. She says, "I think you should talk to your doctor about getting a little something to take the edge off because you're handling a lot of stress right now, honey. It's really not good to not be able to look at your husband."

With this encouragement, I bravely make an appointment with my doctor. She hears me say "laid off" and practically starts writing a prescription for Zoloft without my asking. Apparently, I'm not her first patient with this issue. It's amazing how this little pill dials the stress back enough that I can see how hard this time is for both Gary and me, and that I love my husband, and it's not his fault that a guy as brilliant as he is can't get a job. I've never taken an antidepressant before and am nervous about taking it long-term, so I decide I'll wean myself off it after a month or two. But for now, the lens has been defogged. Regrettably, orgasms are definitely gone, but that is a trade worth making to get my husband back. The irony of a medication taken to help reconnect having that side effect.

It's a good reason to get off the stuff sooner than later. Thank you, dear Elizabeth, for your unconditional love.

I pop by Bel Bambini to see how my single clips are selling and find the basket display is a mess. Most of the ribbons have come off or are untied, and they've been unclipped from the edge of the basket. The best I can do is to fix the ribbons and replace the damaged hang tags. I didn't think customers would be manhandling products in such a nice store.

I call stores and then more stores. I stop by stores. I email stores. I'm not sure what else to do, but no one seems to be buying much.

UNEMPLOYMENT RATE DOESN'T GET THE GOOD NEWS
The unemployment rate refused to believe economists. Despite the Great Recession having ended two months ago, it decided to go up to 9.6%.

August 29, 2009. The most awesome blankyclip review posts on the very popular parenting blog Baby Gizmo.

> I'm always on the lookout for fun, new products that will make great gifts and a new mom's life a little easier. blankyclip is one of those products! blankyclip is a plush animal that doubles as a loose-tension fastening device strong enough to hold a blanket, but gentle enough not to clamp down on tiny fingers.

> We've all been there. You are taking a stroll with your baby and you watch in horror as your baby's blanket falls off the stroller into a mud puddle. Okay, maybe not a mud puddle but definitely on the dirty street or floor. No matter how many times you try to stuff, wrap or tie the blanket around the frame of the stroller, it still seems to break loose and plummet to the ground. Or in my case living in the Windy City, the wind always takes hold of the blanket blowing it across the street or onto the ground to get caught under the dirty stroller wheels!

Momprenuer, Adrienne Alitowski, had the same problem but she did something about it. She created the blankyclip. It is a clip in the form of a cuddly character that is specifically designed to effortlessly hold blankets onto strollers, bouncy seats, swings and more. The blankyclip is available in three adorable characters: a white sheep, a yellow duck and a brown bear. We tried out the cute bears and my two-year-old immediately wanted to hold and play with the toys. He wouldn't let me attach them to his brother's stroller without him checking them out first. Like the company claims, we are pleased to say that these clips are padded and gentle enough not to clamp down on tiny fingers. So, they don't hurt little fingers but do they hold a blanket on the stroller? In one word, yes! We took the two clips and were able to attach a blanket to the stroller easily and it stayed put. The clips even worked on the top of our stroller bassinet to keep the sun from shining in on our little sleeper. The clips also worked on our swing and bouncy seat to prevent the baby from kicking the blanket off.

The clips come in sets of two with a coordinating baby blanket. The included baby blanket is large (30×40 inches) and super soft. The clips and blanket are packaged with a satin ribbon making the set a perfect gift. The set retails for $48 and for more information visit: www.blankyclip.com.

I email this to everyone I know and swear I didn't write it.

Angela sends me a report showing sales are slow, but she includes a message saying she brought blankyclips as a baby shower gift over the weekend and they were "a huge hit!" So, she continues to have faith. She certainly had plenty of products to choose from, and she brought a blankyclip gift set.

The Baby Gizmo review generates some great responses. One is a request to put some blankyclips on consignment in a fancy new boutique opening at the Hollywood & Highland mall. Big foot traffic, hence big potential. At this point, I'll definitely put them in there on consignment. The owner doesn't have the capital to buy merchandise, so this is the only way to get my product in her store.

Gary is happy to take a break from scouring the job sites to write another blankyclip video for our child stars. This one is a musical. The kids sing "blankyclip, blankyclip . . ." to the tune of "Oliver, Oliver!" and speak in horrible English accents about why people should buy my clips to keep their blankets from falling off their strollers. They are absolutely hilarious. Dagny tries to be defiant and do the opposite of what we ask, and that, it turns out, is how to get an amazing performance out of a two-and-a-half-year-old. It feels good to be laughing with Gary and working on a creative project together.

Domo arigato! A Japanese distributor wants to buy blankyclips to sell in Japan. He saw my product at the ABC trade show in Vegas. He wants single clips and gift sets and doesn't have a problem that they are manufactured in China. He's based in Hawaii, and I'm psyched. Now I need to pack up the order of thirty-six gift sets and seventy-two single clips. Feels like blankyclip is starting to gain momentum.

September 2009. Eli, the baby who needed his stroller to be covered with a blanket so he could nap, is going to his first day of kindergarten. School is starting four days late because of the Station Fire, which will turn out to be the largest wildfire in the history of LA County. So much excitement leading up to this big milestone (Kindergarten!) and then the air is too dirty for kids to breathe (Armageddon!). Eli's been going to preschools for years, so this is not a scary day for him. I don't have to make up a story about how I will be "right back" when I say goodbye. He is delighted with his new environment and his very grown-up status. Gary and I are even more delighted he has made it to free education.

Painfully not free is the preschool where Dagny starts her journey of education and independence days later. After I'm there for a few hours to confirm that I am absolutely not meant to be a preschool teacher, I tell Dagny that I need to leave for a little bit but will be back to pick her up. She reaches for me after I give her a kiss and grabs my hair in her little fist. I pry her little fingers away, feeling like a terrible mother for leaving her to take care of an order from Japan.

It's our thirteenth anniversary and we're broke, so it's just out for a drink tonight. Hard to believe it's been eight months and Gary still doesn't have a job. We are sitting at the bar of a fancy hotel on the beach because he knows I love being near the ocean. He also knows what I'm thinking as we watch people around us who seem full of cheer. We don't feel very celebratory, but we toast to better times and take a walk holding hands. Through thick and through thin. It's so much harder to feel joyous during the thin time, but here we are.

ECONOMISTS REPORT STABILIZATION OF ECONOMIC FORECASTS; ALL OTHER HUMANS DISAGREE

Economists, including some at the Federal Reserve, rolled their eyes at the general public when the Consumer Confidence Index didn't skyrocket the way the Fed thought it should. The Fed lashed out, saying, "Come on, what do you want? The rate of layoffs is slowing down." The public responded by griping about an unemployment rate of 9.8% and whining that one out of four of them had a "job loss or layoff in their home" within the last year.

Sales are still going slowly at Buy Buy Baby: eleven units of sheep, ten units of duck, and only one bear so far. Angela sends me the report, and I freak out. She reassures me, "Don't worry! It'll pick up! I've been telling people to register for blankyclips when I'm out walking the floor."

It is disheartening to hear that Lullaby Lane in northern California (my first order at the Vegas show) isn't interested in putting in a reorder. I'm baffled about how to get people to buy this product. When I send it to the blogs, I get fantastic reviews. People tell me they love blankyclips. So far, all orders shipped from my website have been well received. I get great emails from my customers. Darn that pesky CCI. But at least the Japan order gets picked up and is on its way. Little Japanese babies will soon have blankyclips on their strollers! How cool is that?

* * *

September 17, 2009. Angela emails me. The last time I heard from her, she told me that my sales were slow but predicted they'd improve. Now she writes that based on good sales, she's rolling me out to the entire chain: twenty-six more stores. I'm thrilled and terrified, but mostly terrified. So, what else is new? Time to order more clear vinyl bags.

Gary starts moving our furniture around. "We need to turn the living room into a fulfillment warehouse," he says matter-of-factly. Out by the garage, I rip away the plastic bags around each blanket and shake them out to get rid of the loose fuzzies. The driveway looks like it snowed. This is definitely going to be challenging. The order requires almost a thousand vinyl bags. Twelve units of three designs for twenty-six stores means 936 units shipping in seventy-eight case packs (boxes), all packaged by hand. Our hands.

My angel friends offer to help with the packing. They walk into our house and can't believe what they see. Mountains of blankets that need to be rolled and tied with ribbon, piles of ribbon strips, bags of inspected blankyclips, cartons of vinyl bags . . . It's madness, but they jump right in.

We work on the order night and day. Inspecting and cleaning and fixing the blankyclips is so time consuming. Some of them have black threads under the fur that can be seen through the lighter areas. Some don't have enough padding where the two ends pinch down. I have to salvage every usable blankyclip, since so many weren't made correctly. No time to cry over that now.

***

October 2009. Gary cleans out the Public Storage shed (God bless the man) and takes inventory. I'm glad to know my inventory count but troubled that I have no factory lined up for the day when I can put in another order. There are thirty percent fewer sheep clips than the other designs because the factory ran out of my white fabric during production.

THE RIGHT STUFF

After filing for bankruptcy in February 2009 and closing its thirty stores, the baby-gear retailer Right Start reemerged with new owners—and nine stores.

The buyer at Right Start still isn't interested in bringing blankyclip into her chain. When I tell her about the Buy Buy Baby rollout, hoping to pique her interest, she says, "We're dealing with our current inventory, and our holiday section needs attention." I take this to mean that they aren't selling as much of what they have as they thought they would, probably because they're trying to sell thirty stores' worth of merchandise in just nine stores. I have to keep things friendly, but I can certainly make faces at my computer screen. Her initial story was that after the product proved itself in the boutiques she'd be ready to bring me in. Here I am in a large chain store, and she isn't ready. But that was before a bankruptcy entered the equation.

I'm excited about being in the new boutique at the Hollywood & Highland mall, Right Bank Babies. The owner is a creative and savvy businesswoman. Even though my product will be there on consignment, I think it's a great opportunity. The gals working in the store are amazing and very motivated.

CHOOSE YOUR POISON

October 2009 offered a variety of ways to feel sad. If a bank wanted to foreclose on your home, you might've felt the pinch of the foreclosure crisis. Pressure came from lawmakers and economists to halt foreclosures because too many were happening all at once. Or you could've showed up at your job one day in October and discovered it didn't exist any longer. October 2009 saw unemployment reach 10.0%. Or if you had a new product geared toward young children and parents, you might've lamented the fact that Toys "R" Us reported a $67 million loss from August to October.

Here's a fact that is shocking to learn. A chain store vendor (rhymes with Cry Cry Maybe) can have payment terms that look like this: We'll pay you that wholesale price in seventy-five days, and 105 days if the order is shipping to a new store. Oh, and for that store we'll also knock twenty percent off your invoice since we have lots of expenses opening a new store—you know, shelves and lighting—and you, the vendor, should pay for some of those expenses.

On the bright side, we're having a Grand Opening party at Right Bank Babies, and man, is it fun! So much of my business is about me figuring it out on my own, so it feels good to be part of a nice group of women building something together. I do hope that blankyclips sell well here. The clips are being sold individually and also as sets with the blankets. I'll split the sale fifty-fifty with the store.

November 2009. It's a good day when you get an email that says your product is in a photo in a national magazine. Hot Moms Club Emily has done it again: blankyclip is in *Life & Style* magazine! The photo shows Judy Reyes, from the TV show *Scrubs*, standing next to a stroller with a sheep blankyclip gift set in it. The accompanying article is all about her baby shower and the gifts she got. The only issue is that the white sheep blankyclips are hard to see in the photo, and even the pink blanket doesn't show up too well, but I am in *Life & Style*, and this is huge for me. Thank goodness for Emily, yet another blankyclip angel.

And then Angela at Buy Buy Baby rains on the blankyclip parade. She asks if she can reduce my case packs to holding six units instead of twelve. I guess this is so she can order fewer than twelve per design, although she hasn't actually said so. What can I possibly tell her? No? It appears that my $40 baby stroller accessory is not such a hot item.

What *is* hot is a pot I've left on my stove for hours while I am out doing errands. When I enter our duplex, the smoke detector is beeping and the kitchen is enveloped in an acrid cloud. My chimichurri rice from Trader Joe's is charred beyond Peruvian recognition, and the Teflon pot reeks of carcinogens. I am trying to manage being a small business owner and a homemaker and a supportive wife. How am I doing?

ET TU, KOURTNEY?

November 2009. Kourtney Kardashian's baby store, Smooch, open since 2003, officially closed its doors for good. A Kardashian store!

I fly back to New York for my twenty-fifth (gulp!) high school reunion. While I'm there, I pop into the Chelsea Buy Buy Baby store and see that my product is no longer easily found. Now the three gift sets are in the middle of an aisle and all squeezed ridiculously onto a few pegs. I try my best to organize them, but given the tight quarters, they still end up looking like a mess.

I pay a visit to Albee's, which never paid for the six vinyl bags that my friend Randy hand-delivered. I find only two bags. The store is busy, and I'm filled with a sinking feeling when I approach the manager, who tells me, "They haven't been great sellers." Four of them seem to have been, but he moves on to help a customer. The fact that I am standing in his store 3,000 miles away from my home doesn't seem to warrant much more attention from him than that. And the fact that he owes me for the four blankyclip gift sets that he did sell (for $160 retail) doesn't seem to faze him, either.

December 2009. Back in Los Angeles. I'm not sure this is going to work, but I think it would help if Buy Buy Baby put my product in the gift section instead of jamming it into a forgotten corner of the stroller accessory aisle. I call Jim, one of the managers in the Chelsea store, and ask if he could move at least some of the vinyl bags. "I'm not authorized for that," he tells me. "Since a stroller accessories buyer purchased the product, it has to remain in the stroller accessories section." Dang, that buyer thing again. I email Angela and ask about moving some blankyclips into the gift section, and she tells me she can't help me because it's at the store's discretion. I guess we won't be moving into the gift section any time soon.

I'm having a terrible day. I visit Right Bank Babies at the mall and am horrified. My product has been trashed. It's the Chelsea Buy Buy Baby and Bel Bambini all over again, but worse. The blankyclips in the basket display have been torn apart. The blankets in the gift sets have clearly been unrolled and sloppily retied—with twine. Most of the hang tags have been crushed or removed. The whole thing looks awful, and when I do an inventory count, many pieces are missing, yet they've not been sold. Here I am wondering why the product isn't selling, and it turns out it's just walking out the door or being destroyed so that it *can't* sell. I want to be in this store, but this is ridiculous. How can they have let things fall apart like this? And what in the world are customers doing with the hang tags?

Now that I have a couple of magazine mentions, I'm thinking it would be a good time to hit up *Cookie* magazine. They were at the Vegas trade show, and I wanted them to notice my press kit there, to no avail.

I email my friend and free publicist Brooke to see if she can pursue them. "I would," she says, "except *Cookie* magazine is out of business." Wow. The amazing lifestyle magazine for the modern mother is no more.

WE'RE #24!

In the twenty-four years that ABC News has tracked its Consumer Comfort Index (not to be confused with the Conference Board's Consumer Confidence Index—actually, it was likely *designed* to be confused with the Conference Board's more respected CCI), 2009 went down as the worst year on record. The nearly 50,000 people who lost their jobs at Pfizer, Merck, and Johnson & Johnson alone attested to the fact that their consumer comfort was indeed quite low. Even attorneys pleaded guilty to having an awful year. 2009 was the worst year ever for layoffs at law firms, with over 12,000 losing their jobs.

It looks like I may have found a new factory in China as a result of my trip to northern California to meet the American part-owner. They say they can make samples of my three current designs and also an elephant and a hippo at $1.78 per clip, and for five more cents they can add a squeak mechanism to the belly so the blankyclips can be squeak toys too. Awesome. The price for the vinyl bag version to sell to the big stores—blanket wrapped with ribbon, two blankyclips, and the cardboard insert—would come to $10.96.

These are prices that may work when I am able to sell on my website for $48. Less so when I sell to a boutique for $24 wholesale, but absolutely not if a big box store wants to carry them for $25 retail, as Angela suggested. In one of their new stores, where I'm losing an additional twenty percent, I won't get back what I pay the factory, even without shipping or any of my other costs. The only way to keep the company going if I'm selling for those prices is to have a line of credit or investment. Of course, putting in an order for 500,000 blankyclips would bring my price down too.

It's not the job of a lifetime, but it's a job, and Gary takes it. He starts doing some part-time consulting and again is driving about sixty miles each way for it. Almost ten months without work have taken their toll on his confidence and our finances. Neither easily mended, but it's a start. We both spend our days pushing forward with all our might, but at night in bed the tears tell a different story. His and mine. I want to hear him say it's all going to be okay and he'll soon have a better job, but after all these months he knows those words would ring hollow. We lie there next to each other in silence, the kids asleep and unaware of the uncertainty between us.

I get a boost when a company in Atlanta called Larry Lucas offers to represent blankyclips in the Southeast region. Graphic designer Patty helps me with a new sell sheet. I have to add the single blankyclip option, as I now have sales reps. My first reps! And all because my friend Elizabeth visited her friend, and her friend's sister-in-law is a rep. Crazy! They also want my brochures but with their contact info on them. I'm excited that now I won't be the only person trying to sell this damn product. (I mean, this adorable invention that I've been nurturing for six years.)

> **WAIT! SOMETHING—NOT UNEMPLOYMENT—GOES UP!**
> Unemployment held steady at 9.9% (It went down a tenth of a percent since October). But something did go up. Prices! The Consumer Price Index increased 2.7% over the past 12 months. What the heck, no one had any money to buy stuff anyway.

Time to bid goodbye to 2009. Unmet expectations bleed into visions of a new year that will bring us the work and the sales and the success we are longing for.

I call Gary to tell him that although we had high hopes for an adorable preschool photo of our three-year-old daughter, we will not be seeing one. When the photographer told her she was next, she refused to let him take her picture. She tells me after school, "I didn't like his face." My husband laughs with me about this in a way no one else can. We wonder together how it is possible that in this same week our six-year-old son accepted an invitation to stand up and sing with a band at the farmer's market. With his own mic! We are so in love with the perfect way each of them is.

I go to the post office to Express Mail a couple hundred of my brochures to Atlanta with stickers on the back showing the new sales rep info. Next, I'll need to reach out to all of the individual reps and introduce myself and get them samples.

My Japan guy is interested in putting in a large order for some department stores in Japan, but only if I can drop-ship the merchandise to his Japanese warehouse directly from my factory in China. That way he won't have to pay such high duties and shipping costs. If only. At the moment, I don't have a factory, and I don't have the funds to put in a new production order. Where I have product is in Los Angeles. It's lovely to imagine the day when I'm able to send him product from China, but that day isn't here, so I have to put him off.

The first orders come in from my Southeast sales reps . . . all from small boutiques, for not many units, but I'll take it. The fact that I had nothing to do with these sales is something of a miracle. Buyers came to the Larry Lucas showroom in Atlanta, saw my product, and put in orders!

READ IT AND WEEP

January 2010. Borders closed its 738th bookstore, leaving 511 out of the 1,249 they once had. This after the end of 2009, when the U.S. economy grew at its fastest pace in six years. Goldman Sachs did what Borders couldn't—report an increase in profits for 2009. Retailers not called Borders strutted around brandishing their 2009 holiday receipts, which were marginally better than in 2008. U.S. Treasury Secretary Timothy Geithner told everyone to settle down and not pop the champagne corks just yet. He reminded them that 2008 was the worst holiday season in, like, forever, and maybe not the bar to measure against. Also, those 4,000 new jobs created in November 2009—well, the economy lost 85,000 more in December, and it was hard to get a recovery going when almost one in ten Americans were still out of work.

Samples arrive from the factory in China with the American part-owner. The new elephant and hippo are both really cute. I ask around for recommendations on which animal to pick, and a friend who works at Disney says, "Elephants are really trending now, although by the time you get your elephant made, things could change."

February 8, 2010. Oh happy day! Modernmom.com, the celebrity-run parenting blog, has given me a fabulous review. It couldn't be more positive.

> How many times has your baby blanket fallen off your child during a walk and ended up on the dirty floor? I can tell you that this happens to me all the time. Wind blows, blanket goes, and now it is dirty and germy. I love this simple and easy way to keep that blanket on your baby or toddler while they are sleeping or relaxing in the stroller or car seat. Such a great idea and simple concept.
>
> blankyclip "clips" the blanket on to the stroller or car seat so it doesn't fly off. Adorable little stuffed animal clips are easy to squeeze and attach to your stroller. It's cute, it helps block the sun from your baby's precious face, and

it won't let that blanket slip off your little "kicker." They attach on to the side of your stroller, and make a good toy for your toddler to hold when boredom sets in.

$15 at www.blankyclip.com

———

Am I on a roll or what? Five years after I first started trying to get them, my trademarks for the name blankyclip and my logo are now officially registered! Henry sends me the good news that I can now officially use the R in a circle next to the word blankyclip.

Within moments of hearing this news, I get an invoice from Henry's office. Couldn't I have at least a moment of joy?

It's interesting how quickly things work once you have some good buzz going. A TV producer at Fox31 in Denver emails me to request samples and press info so she can put blankyclip in her product idea segment. She adds a personal note asking where I've been the past nine years when she's been having children. Lovely words of support along with my first TV exposure!

Angela sends me the latest sales report. It isn't great. She suggests that I lower my retail price to $29.99 to move the product faster, but then I'd owe the stores $5 per unit on what they've already bought. An order from a Buy Buy Baby store in Schererville, Indiana, comes in but for the reduced case pack, six units instead of twelve.

The other six in my life is Eli, and his six is one that feels very complete and big. Today he's having his first piano lesson. As his little fingers explore the keys on our $75 upright Kimball from a thrift store, the notes connect him to a family tradition of music education. (I got to shoot that music video thanks to a childhood studying the cello and piano.) They fill my heart and our home with delight, and for a moment I forget about that other six.

CLIPPED

March 2010. Gary writes a funny blankyclip video spoofing the Old Spice commercial with the guy who ends up shirtless on a horse on a beach. In our case, Eli's not shirtless, and it's Dagny who ends up on a (rocking) horse. Eli has all his lines ("Hello, Ladies") down like a pro, but we're shooting in our yard, and take after take has to be redone because of a car or a loud noise outside, and then there's the technical issue of having the set disappear, like in the ad. By the zillionth time Eli says "Hello, Ladies," his voice is cracking from stress, and he loses it. No shot works, and we scrap the whole project and pray that Eli will forgive us.

I decide to try catalogues. I've heard mixed things about selling to a catalogue, but it might be great exposure. I submit blankyclip to the *One Step Ahead* catalogue. I hear from *Land of Nod* that they're not interested. There are plenty more catalogues, though.

If I lived in Denver, I could watch the piece on blankyclip that's airing today, but I don't so I can't. When I try to watch it on the web, the link they send me doesn't work. But as a result of this airing, I get a nice spike in visits to my website, and the producer says she got a great response to my product. Good to hear.

I listen to a guy giving a free publicity seminar and like his idea of approaching my hometown newspaper. It stirs up memories of walking on wet dewy grass on the occasional mornings I helped my brother with his paper route delivering the *Standard Star*. It would help if that newspaper I grew up with still existed. Oh well. So much for pitching the charming article about the hometown girl who invented a baby product and is now looking for people to buy it.

Closing down must be contagious. The maternity and baby trade show that my mom friend started, Mom2B, is closing its doors. They're hoping someone will buy their brand, but it's just too expensive to run the show and they can't afford to keep going. It was getting too hard to get vendors (i.e., people like me) to pay for booth space. I'm sad for my friend, but she did an awesome job with it while it lasted. These are amazing times. (Read "amazing" in an ironic, melancholy kind of way.)

It seems like everyone is hurting for business. Today I get emails from two printing companies, the publicity seminar guy, a movie theater ads guy named Josh, and two other PR companies. Everyone wants *my* business. That's pretty funny.

In an effort to keep my product out there at a time when stores don't seem to be ordering, I ask Juvenile Shop if they'd put a basket of single blankyclips in their store on consignment. They say yes, so I bring them a basket with four of each design. The buyer, Erin, tells me to contact her in a month, and we'll see how they do. I offer to bring more of the blanket gift sets, but she doesn't respond, even though she sold the six sets she bought way back when. At this point, I just want to make sure blankyclips are still in her store, and consignment is the only way.

I meet with Josh about advertising in movie theaters, which is ridiculously expensive and not happening. When I tell him that I have to grow my company before I can afford to advertise in theaters, he tells me about Julie who works on getting products into big chain stores. She sounds fabulous, and how soon can I meet her? He gets in touch with her and tells her about my product/website. After she checks it out, she says she'd love to talk to me and is definitely interested in helping get me to the next level. What a promising connection.

I'm off to Right Bank Babies to restock. Things look much better over there, and they're selling lots of blankyclips. The gals there are great and believe in the product.

I ship a funny order today, from a Larry Lucas sales rep: only duck blankyclips, going to the Peabody Hotel in Memphis, Tennessee. The hotel is famous for the ducks that walk around the lobby every day.

We haven't even met yet, but after just one phone call, Julie emails me to say that she got great feedback from Amazon.com. Are you kidding me? She's a total go-getter and is in love with my product. Then she sends me a Sales Representative contract in which she asks for $25,000 a year, plus eight percent commission. I gulp. I gasp. I call her to say that this is really beyond where I'm at right now. She says she completely understands. I should send her some revised numbers, but basically she sees no problem in getting my product into all the major retailers throughout the United States. I'm really digging this woman. We set up a coffee meeting at a Starbucks in West Covina.

* * *

April 2010. How many meetings in Starbucks have I had for my company? It's the new way people connect in the small business world. Anyway, it's great to meet someone who's so passionate about what she does and who sees such potential for blankyclips. She's working for a few other clients and has just gotten them into Rite Aid and Duane Reade, and she's the real deal. I give her some samples and my press kit (she loves all the design work), and then the next step is to get our contract ironed out so she can work full force on getting blankyclips into the major chains. I'm feeling so good about the potential of this new partnership that I treat myself to a sushi lunch.

It's a relief when she agrees to my terms: $6,000 yearly when a revenue stream becomes available, but start with ten percent commission and then drop to eight percent when her salary kicks in. She talks faster than my brother, who's always been the fastest talker I know. She tells me she'd like to be called Director of North American Operations. No problem.

Julie sees the future of blankyclips as just a pair of clips without the blanket. I have to figure out what packaging for the big chain stores would look like for two clips hanging on a peg and how to make all this happen without a budget to hire a packaging designer, but I think she's right about going for the lower-end market and forgetting about the gift/boutique look. I'll have much less of a profit margin this way, but it's clear that I need to lower the cost of my product. The $40 version at Buy Buy Baby isn't exactly flying off the pegs.

THAT'S ENTERTAINMENT!

Movie Gallery, Inc., owner of the DVD rental companies Hollywood Video, Game Crazy, and Movie Gallery, announced it was closing all of its stores. At one point, they had about 4,700 of them in North America. In a separate but related news story, the unemployment rate—in spite of the fact that the Great Recession belonged in history textbooks along with the Alamo and the *Titanic*—stubbornly refused to fall below 9.9%.

I visit Babies "R" Us to check out what's going on in the stroller accessories department and see how things are packaged. I notice that many of the brands that used to be hanging on those pegs have been replaced by basically the same product in the "Especially for Baby" generic line that Babies "R" Us manufactures. So, you get your product into their store, and after a while Babies "R" Us figures out how to manufacture it themselves, and then they stop selling your version. Much cheaper for them to make it themselves and sell it for a lower price. They make more money because there's no pesky brand to take away some of their profit margin. A win for everyone but the small businesses (or not so small businesses) they used to carry.

I go back and forth on tweaks to the new factory's samples. Once I'm happy with their quality, they send their final quote: $2.13 per blankyclip. Do they mean for the pair? No, they mean per clip. I'm screwed.

Julie sends me a profit and loss sheet that spells out what the costs to sell to the big chains are going to be and how to figure out my profit margin. She shows me that if the stores sell the two clips for $19.99 and I pay $4 for the clips to be made, I will have a slim profit margin but that it is doable.

Here's why the math doesn't add up for me right now. Basically, if it costs me $80,000 to make 40,000 clips (rounding down to $2 per clip), which is 20,000 sets, the profit at the end of the day is going to be around $40,000. Why? If I'm getting $10 for wholesale, then one percent off for returns, that brings us to $9.90. Then there's the cost of warehousing, freight, Julie's commission, etc., which leaves me with about $6. If I sell 20,000 units, that comes to $120,000. And if it cost me $80,000 to produce those 20,000 units, that leaves me with a gross profit of about $40,000. Lots of numbers to explain that I don't have enough money to put in a new order and cover the expenses of running the company. My cost of goods has to be much lower for this to work.

But at this point we have a small order from Amazon for only six sets of each design, so there's no harm in getting started there to see how things go. It's a little scary that if it does go well, I'll need to fulfill orders and I don't have a ton of inventory and the factory's giving me prices that are too high—but what the hell.

Julie also has an idea about just putting the clips on a cardboard backing and not using any kind of poly or vinyl bag, which is interesting. There's the problem of dirt getting on the blankyclips, but at the same time the customer can get a feel for what the product is and how it works. I'm sure I could make the cardboard design look great with all my photos, and then all I need to figure out is how to attach the clips to this cardboard backing. But at least the whole thing can easily be hung on a peg from the hole cut out on top. I invite Julio, the package designer from Stila Cosmetics, to discuss this idea over lunch. He's excited to be working with me again. Such a nice guy and so talented.

May 2010. The fun just doesn't stop. Today I get an obnoxious email from Larry Lucas, the owner of the sales rep company in the Southeast. He tells me that he's heard from some boutique stores that don't want to carry my product because it's also in Buy Buy Baby. He has a list of questions about how much product I sold to Buy Buy Baby. Was the sale so big it won't matter to me when the smaller children's stores quit ordering? Can I give the same pricing to the boutiques? And finally, he asks me the best question of all: "How much longer do you think independent stores can survive?"

Suddenly I'm responsible for the fact that people are turning to the larger chain stores because of lower prices? Me? But as a matter of fact, an order for $30,000 of product was big enough for me not to question being in Buy Buy Baby for a second. Furthermore, the pricing is different for the boutique gift sets, which are $8 more, not in the vinyl bag, and meant to attract a higher-end consumer. Buy Buy Baby doesn't even carry the single clips, so that's not an issue. When I signed with Larry Lucas, I made it clear that I was in the Buy Buy Baby chain, so this is completely unfair and unprofessional of him. I'm not to blame for the fact that boutiques are not doing well in this economy.

I'm still boiling a few hours later when I'm greeted with a happy email informing me that my second patent will be issued in a couple of weeks. My fabulous lawyer, Henry, tells me to add this new number—7,716,793—to any product labeling or packaging that I'm using, so as to "increase damages in case of a would-be infringer." So, in the morning, I'm the cause of the demise of small children's stores, and in the afternoon, I'm protecting myself from bigger fish that might want to infringe on my property. What a day.

10

One Letter Changes Everything

RED IS THE NEW BLACK

From 2008 to 2010, 200,000 small businesses in the United States closed because they were in the red, eliminating 3,000,000 jobs.

A blankyclip has so many components, and there's really no place to cut corners to get my cost down. The inner clip is an expense. Then the foam. Then the plush animal design that needs to be sewn together. The bellies get stuffed with another foam. There's embroidery on the faces. Why didn't I invent baby leg warmers? A single tube of stretchy fabric. The American part-owner of the new factory complains that Washington, D.C. is pressuring Beijing to allow the RMB (Chinese currency) to increase in value, which will cause manufacturing costs to rise even more before the end of the year. He says the only way to achieve a considerable price reduction is with a major product redesign, like not covering the entire clip with the plush. I have two patents for the product to function as it does now. I feel very out of control.

Julio tells me that the packaging vendor he was hoping to talk to about making a cardboard header for blankyclip is no longer in business. As he puts it, "They went under." What an expression. But he's going to continue working on the art design and will try to have something for me soon.

San Diego Family Magazine's May issue is my favorite of all because it's the one that features blankyclip. I got a great review. When they asked moms to give my product a test run, the moms rated it nine out of ten!

June 2010. No! After waiting so long for Julio to put together a design for my header card, he emails me that he won't be able to work on the project after all. His computer crashed, and he's dealing with getting it repaired, and that's about all he can handle. Now what? I have to find someone to do this for me fast. I write Julie and give her the bad news. She's going to try to come up with a designer for me.

I get the sweetest email from a new store in Alabama. The owner writes, "I can't wait to start carrying the clips! I think they are one of the smartest inventions ever!" These kinds of messages lift my mood and give me strength to carry on for another day.

The problem with needing to hire a packaging designer is that they require money. Lots of it. Julio's rate was the angel rate. Julie sends me a link to a design firm that is way over my budget, so I get busy looking on the internet and I find my guy. He lives in North Palm Beach, Florida, has his own business, and is willing to cut me a deal: $500!

All this different pricing is crazy-making. We're setting up a two-clip pack on Amazon for $24.99, but in the boutiques it's still $15 for an individual clip. The direction of my company is to lower prices, but

I can't do that yet for the boutique orders which are so small. This is definitely something that worries me after getting yelled at via email by Larry Lucas about the Buy Buy Baby pricing, but I've certainly seen different prices for the same product before depending on where I'm shopping.

Goodness, the setup for Amazon doesn't end! First there was the Vendor Terms & Conditions form, then the Vendor Orientation form. Now there's an enormous spreadsheet with questions to fill out about my product. How do I know the maximum suggested weight for a child using this product? I go with thirty-five pounds, since that's how much Dagny weighs. Next is figuring out how to upload pictures to their site. Julie's waiting to hear back from their customer service department in India with answers to our emailed questions. Why can't we just *call* someone to get answers to our questions?

My Florida designer is awesome. He's done wonders with the front of the card where the blankyclips will be hanging and there's not much space for information. He's chosen to use a picture of baby Dagny sitting in her stroller holding a blankyclip with the pink blanket hanging to block the sun that's hitting her face, but secured to the top by another blankyclip and not entirely covering the stroller. He says showing an awake and happy child will be more appealing to a customer than showing a covered stroller. I'm selling my product as a clip and as a toy, and this shot shows both uses. Also, my guy has switched the white sheep blankyclip Dagny was holding in the original photo for a much more visible brown bear. It's amazing what can be done to alter a photo. We did not get a shot of her holding a bear clip, yet he created one.

The tagline on the front is: *A baby-safe clip that's also a toy!* He's put markers for the holes where the zip ties will go through to secure the clips, and a marker for the hole on top to hang the package on a peg. The color palate on the front is yellow and green. It looks like a baby product, and it looks professional, and I love it! On the back there are more shots of the product, and my guy has taken the covered stroller shot with the ecru blanket and made the blanket blue so you can see the yellow duck blankyclips. How has this never occurred to me or anyone else I've worked with before? Such a great idea, and now the picture works so much better. There are descriptions of why to buy the product, and there's a note from me, the mom inventor, to personalize the whole thing, with my signature no less. Amazing what you can do with a scanner.

There have been lots of typos to fix and little tweaks with the captions, plus adding Made in China and adding room for the UPC code. When I ask my dear designer to tone down the shade of blue on the blanket, he hits the wall and lets me know that he cannot be expected to keep making so many changes for $500. We have a conversation, and he calms down and tones down the blue.

Two patents are great, but we are going for a third, the last chunk of my original child-safe fastening device patent. Henry thinks we'll get it, and he says the more claims I have patented, the stronger my case for going after any future baby-safe fastening devices that someone might try to manufacture. I've come this far. Hard to stop now, so we file a continuation, and there goes another grand!

Julie suggests that we make the picture of the baby in the stroller on the front of the card look more unisex. Since we're not going to remove Dagny from the shot, the only other option is switching the color of the blanket from pink to . . . what? Dagny is wearing a green outfit, and there's plenty of green in the card already. Yellow wouldn't show up strongly, so my designer tries orange, and it looks great. It adds a nice splash of color, and now the bear blankyclips pop out even more. Thankfully, he was willing to make these changes.

One month later, we have the final files to send to the printer. Now I just have to find a printer and some cardboard stock that's thick enough to hold the blankyclips without buckling.

July 2010. Julie's in a hurry to get my mock-ups printed as she has meetings with drugstore.com and Whole Foods and wants to be "retail-ready" to present to Target. All I can do is keep pushing and hope it gets done soon.

I follow up with a boutique called Twinkle Twinkle Little Store in Monrovia, California, to see if they want to put in a reorder, and I learn that the store has closed. The owner is sweet to let me know that she loves my product and that it sold well for her. And another store bites the dust.

Gary's connection to the venture capitalists that own Stila leads me to yet another new factory, and I send them blankyclip samples to review. They have some questions about the dog design. Ahem, that's a bear. But they're going to make me their own samples, and they think they can beat the pricing quotes I've had so far. I hope so.

The header card mock-ups arrive looking gorgeous. Now I can overnight one to Julie in Seattle so she can show it to the buyers she's meeting. This is a huge opportunity.

July 19, 2010. I get a fabulous review on a great mommy blog called Gearheadmom.com.

blankyclip: A Lovie's Best Friend

I was given the opportunity as the mother of a fresh baby boy to review blankyclip, the "only plush toy that doubles as a loose tension clip, specifically designed to hold blankets onto strollers, bouncy seats, swings, etc." I figured why not, as I had only recently realized that I misplaced my favorite Little Giraffe blanket and figured that it most likely fell off of my stroller or car seat. Before the clips came in the mail I checked out the website and while I thought they were cute and smart and seemed to be useful, honestly my first thought was, can I picture myself using these? Like, am I too "cool" to have a duckie or lamb or a teddy bear clip hanging off of my gear?

We took them for a spin at the Zoo. If there is anywhere to road-test baby gear for a stroller, the Zoo is the place. Stroller central. I used the little duckie blankyclips to clip the lightweight but warm and soft blanket to the car seat in our jogger. Because we live in wet climate, the clips were very effective at keeping the drizzle from coming through the crack between the car seat canopy and our jogger canopy. If the sun were shining, they would have been just as effective! blankyclip success!

The next opportunity to road-test these was on our car trip home from the Zoo. They worked great to secure the blanket over the window when the sun was at the wrong angle! I also found an opportunity to utilize them during one of my 4-1/2-yr-old's play dates. I used the clips to secure blankets for a "fort" they were stringing across the living room. Success! Speaking of my 4-1/2-year-old— my daughter often carts them off to play with and I have to search for them among her "stuffies".

Oh, and I must not forget the latest use, I used the clips to secure the blanket over my shoulder at the park when I forgot my "hooter hider". I obviously got over my worries about being too "cool"! But that goes out the door with a second child pretty darn quickly.

Snapshot:

✓ This blankyclip = great multi-tasker: keeps blankets and forts secure, while not totally crushing your cool-cred.

✓ Easy to use and not pinchy.

✓ The prices for the blankyclips vary: $15.00 for one clip or $48.00 for a set of two with a blanket. After polling many momma friends, we have decided that the price of the clip/blanky combo is on the higher side for gear, but a great idea for a shower present.

This writer hit upon every single aspect of why all moms with babies need some blankyclips—also useful for forts! The question is how to get this kind of a review to affect sales.

I'm sure I would've heard back from Julie if the buyers were interested, but I still email her hoping to get some response. I'm clearly not a priority. If I were a priority, it wouldn't be impossible to get hold of her. Finally, she lets me know that the buyers loved blankyclip and thought it was innovative. So innovative that they didn't put in a single order, though drugstore.com wants to see it again in six months. The buyer at Whole Foods also thought it was great, but he's looking to add only "high-turn items" at this time. Why can't blankyclips be high-turn items? It's depressing to keep hearing how great my product is when no one is buying it.

Julie thinks I should put together a PowerPoint presentation that she can show the buyers for the big retailers. She has another client who did this and has been getting a good response. This way I can spell out exactly what blankyclips are and why the buyers should be buying them, and they can have something to show the folks in their department if they need further approval in order to move forward. She sends me a copy of what another client has put together. It's okay, but I'm sure I can create something much better.

I get another fun email from Larry Lucas, my Southeast reps, letting me know that it isn't going to work out for them to represent my line anymore. The consensus is that my product is just too expensive.

Amazon gets back to me saying they still need to do two more advanced shipping notice (ASN) tests and one invoice test. I'm also having issues with the photos I sent them. There's no main image coming up for the blankyclip page, and when you click on the three different designs, only the sheep comes up. Also, they've put blankyclips in the toy category but not in the stroller accessory category. I'd like to be in both. I certainly hope they can fix all this quickly, as I shipped the first order to them today.

Amazon vendor central emails me a salad of letters and numbers. The 810 EDI integration is currently stalled. Test 856 for the Purchase Order Number listed below was successful, but the ASN test was not. I feel like I'm on a Star Trek mission, and it's not going well.

Gary and I make a PowerPoint presentation for Julie to show the buyers at the big chains. It tells the story of why the product is needed and why it's a product they need to order. It's got facts and photos and personality. We have so much fun being creative together, and I'm pleased with our work. Julie is too. She's excited to send it off to Target and Kohl's.

The three boxes of blankyclips arrive at the Amazon warehouse in Whitestown, Indiana, and we're still figuring out how to solve all the vendor central issues. Payment terms with Amazon are Net 90. Three months before they pay after an order has shipped. Apparently, I don't really need this money.

EVERYTHING'S COMING UP ROSES . . .

The U.S. Commerce Department released stats showing that the economy shrank by 4.1 percent during the Great Recession, which made it a greater recession than everyone (except the actual human beings living in it) thought. But stop looking in the rearview, people! The International Monetary Fund raised global economic growth forecasts for this year from 4.2% to 4.6%. The stock markets liked that bit of news and ended the week of July 9 with their strongest gains in a year—over 5% for the week alone! The U.S. Fed suggested that the country's financial market, while still fragile, was definitely getting stronger. Yes! Finally!

Our next video is an absolute masterpiece. We shoot it with our kids, this time playing "blankyclip superheroes." They fly in to rescue a struggling mom (played by a willing six-year-old friend of Eli's) whose blanket has fallen off her stroller. Then they all start rapping about blankyclips in their rapper gear. "You put your b with your lanky, you put your c with your lip. You got the only plush toy that doubles as a clip!" We put this new video on my website and watch it over and over with the kids. If cuteness could rescue the economy, we'd be in clover.

———

August 2, 2010. An order comes in from a store in Albuquerque, New Mexico. Julie submits blankyclip to Target. Target passes.

And not because they don't like the product or don't see it selling. They actually think "the product is very unique and fun in nature." They pass because it's a single item and it's challenging for them to work with single-item suppliers. Julie tells them that I have three SKUs and there are more on the way. This doesn't change anything because it's still one item from their perspective. The buyer explains to Julie that there used to be more buyers at Target, but they've made big cuts. Now he has so many vendors to keep track of that he can't bring anyone on if they don't have a whole line or range of products. The new, new factory tells me that samples are on the way, but what's the point?

. . . BUT EVERY ROSE HAS ITS THORNS

The U.S. Fed started using terms like "modest pace" when describing the economic recovery. The British government admitted that the recovery would continue to be "choppy" as prices remained high. Even Sarah, Duchess of York, faced possible bankruptcy—the first for a member of the Royals. And China suggested that things weren't all hunky-dory by reporting that its manufacturing output shrank to its slowest rate in a year and a half—an indication that maybe the rest of us weren't in the mood to buy more stuff.

I swear I've seen single company products at Target. How on earth did they manage to get in the door? I head to Target and look at the products in the stroller accessory aisle. There's one called Mommy Hook, and it's the only product I see from that company. I go home and look them up, and on their website they list their distributors in various countries and around the world. Now I see that I need a distributor. I decide to reach out to their U.S. distributor about blankyclip.

I contact Brian, VP of Sales and Marketing at Keen Distribution. He's interested in learning more about blankyclip and wants me to send him my retail presentation and a sample. I decide to ask Angela at Buy Buy Baby about Keen, and she tells me they're a great company. She buys Mommy Hook and Bumbo seats from them.

Why am I such an idiot? I asked Angela about Keen so she'd think I might be in negotiations with them and I'd look good in her eyes. The exact same day I email her about Keen, she cancels all remaining open orders. She says they have too much product on hand and that sales are poor. I got on her radar, and she looked up my sales record. I should have stayed off her radar.

Amazon orders six more bear sets, which is nice but too small to get too excited about. Ten boxes ship to Buy Buy Baby stores and for their website. Fortunately, these purchase orders weren't open when Angela told me to cancel future orders. I'll need this money when it comes in.

The samples from the new, new factory need a lot of work. The arms aren't right. The head isn't right. The belly and the inner foam aren't right. It's exhausting to keep explaining all this from the other side of the planet.

Brian from Keen Distribution receives the samples I sent. He says he's traveling and will get back to me next week. I wait with bated breath. Once I get a distributor, I'll focus on how I'll afford to order more blankyclips from the new factory or the new, new factory.

On a trip to visit family in New York, I stop by the Chelsea Buy

Buy Baby, and this time it's beyond shocking what has happened to my blankyclips. At first, I can't even find them. I ask a manager, and he scrunches up his nose like he's thinking hard but has no idea what I'm talking about. A second manager does know, and he takes me deep inside the stroller accessories section to the end of a very congested area that you wouldn't find yourself in unless you meant to. My blankyclips are there, looking useless and forgotten, bags dirty and piled on top of each other. There are so many left-behind-looking products jammed into this little space that it's no wonder sales have pretty much stopped. I wouldn't want to buy a blankyclip gift set either. But it's not even worth talking to anyone about why my product has been shoved into this area. I know why: $39.99 was too expensive, and it didn't sell, and then they gave up on me.

***

September 2010. Today Brian passes on blankyclip. He tells me that it's a cute product but that "the group consensus was not strong enough to move forward at this time. Best of luck!" I really had visions of growing the business this way. If the big stores require distributors, then I clearly need one, so I start digging around Google. Then I go back to the Mommy Hook website to see what distributors they use in other markets, and I decide to contact the company in Mexico. I write to the woman there in Spanish and give her my pitch as best I can. I speak Spanish better than I write it, but I write it anyway. About an hour later she responds. She likes my product and wants to know more. Prices. Country of origin. Can she see a sample?

And because why not, I email the president of Mommy Hook to see if he can help me in my search for a distributor. I figure it's worth a shot, and there's nothing to lose by asking. Two hours later he writes me back. We're going to talk tomorrow.

When I ask Brian at Keen for more feedback on why they passed, he tells me that there were two primary concerns: the price point was too high, and they viewed it as a single product. He says they're seeing retailers reduce their numbers of vendors and take minimal risks. A lack of brand presence when competing against the big manufacturers who offer a brand statement within a category is also a big challenge. This is great information. I ask him, if he thinks that $19.99 for two clips is still too high, how low must I go? I would so appreciate his input on pricing.

"We should touch base at the show," he says.

The show he's referring to is none other than the ABC Kids Expo in Las Vegas where he assumes I'll be exhibiting. I wasn't planning to go, but guess what? I am now. I just need to figure out how to get a badge to get myself in.

When I call the president of Mommy Hook, he tells me, "I started selling my product in Australia and New Zealand, and because we were doing well in those territories, I was approached by Keen to be our U.S. distributor." He recommends I try to get into markets outside of the U.S. "That will show the viability of your product," he says. "It's easier to sell outside of the U.S. than it is to start out selling here." Wow. The call is short but very helpful, though I'm jealous of his success.

<hr />

In what might be a sign that I've been at this for too long, I have an appointment with a psychic to discuss the future of blankyclip. She says, "I like your product. You should try to get it into big stores." I don't want to admit how far I drove to hear her say this to me. I did consult a psychic one other time in my life, years ago in Queens, but that's a story for later.

In a big email blast, I let people know that in light of current economic conditions I have lowered the prices of blankyclips. Gift sets are now $39.99 and the single clips are $12.50.

I continue to focus on distributors. My Mexico gal saw the Power-

Point retail presentation and now wants more samples. A Canadian company wants to see the PowerPoint. I'm working it. Since things have fallen apart with Julie, I think my new plan of getting into areas outside the U.S. is going to be my best bet.

Hard to believe, but I'm talking to Right Start again. My contact, Jamie, is no longer with the company. They're now based in Denver. Lots of changes going on over there, but the new folks want to see samples.

Unbelievable. Buy Buy Baby sends me a payment that's short $629, which is accounted for as a "Hold Dollar Chargeback." What on earth is that? I find out that Angela has issued it against my account until they sell more merchandise. So, because my product hasn't sold well, they've decided not to pay me for it? Apparently, they can do this because they are a huge company, and how could I possibly fight them? There's nothing in their Vendor Relations Guide stating that they can do it, and I was counting on this money. They put in an order, I shipped them that order, but now they're not paying for it because sales are poor. Isn't that stealing? After about twelve phone calls, I do manage to collect $69 owed by a small boutique called Mila, but I'm still fuming over the Buy Buy Baby $629.

WTF?

September 2010. Harley-Davidson employees in Wisconsin agreed to a freeze of their own pay and a slash in the workforce so that the rest of their jobs didn't leave the state. U.S. banks set a new record for the home repossession rate, with 1.2 million homes this year. Another 3.2 million American homes remained in foreclosure proceedings. The U.S. poverty rate hit a 15-year high: 14.3% of Americans—almost 44 million of us—lived in poverty. To put that in perspective, 44 million was more than the number of people living in Texas (26 million) or California (38 million) or even the entire country of Canada (35 million). It was as if everyone in California lived in poverty and then everyone in Arizona (6 million) joined them. Here was the WTF part: during the third quarter of 2010 (July, August, and September), U.S. corporations posted the highest profits in history. Something like $1.7 trillion.

The Canada distributor wants me to send more samples so he can show them to some stores and some of their "test moms."

An order comes in on my website, and where it says, "How did you hear about blankyclip?" the customer writes, *Baby Bargains*. This is the book I have wanted to be in for years, the book that new mom was studying voraciously on my first visit to Buy Buy Baby, the book that was my buying bible. I run to Barnes and Noble to get a copy, and there on page 520 is a wonderful mention of my product and website. I could cry. I write the author of the book to say how grateful I am for the mention and that it led to a sale today. She writes back and tells me to "keep up the good work!"

Today I'm sending six sheep blankyclips to Sydney, Australia! A pregnant woman there finds me by doing a Google search on blanket clips. She writes, "I was hoping that in the years since I had my first kid there would be something on the market now better than hair clips!" She also says that she won't need the blanket since it's so hot in the summertime when she's having her baby, and she'll be using a light muslin wrap.

PUTTING THE "BUST" IN BLOCKBUSTER

September 23, 2010. Once the proud owner of 9,000 stores and employer of 60,000 human beings, Blockbuster, the video rental company, filed for bankruptcy. Unemployment remained stagnant at 9.5%.

October 2010. Today's fun email is from Buzz Girls, a company I sent free blankyclips to for a possible product placement on an episode of *Beverly Hills, 90210*. They send me shots of the blankyclips cutely displayed on a table in their "trunk show set." Not that I expect it to create much buzz for my company, but I figured it was worth sending some product to people on a hit TV show. Especially since, in 1999, I had a blast playing Joyce in one episode. I would never have guessed that this would be how I'd return to the show.

Inspired by my sale in Australia, I do some digging on distributors there and come across a company named Bambini International. I email to ask if I can send them my retail presentation, and get a response saying my contact is out of the country. This administrative assistant and I begin a nice correspondence, and after a few emails I find out that her boss, Ken, will be in Vegas at the ABC Expo. Now I really need to be there. Especially since his assistant is setting up a meeting for us while he's at the show.

My friend who has a pregnancy clothing business says she'd be happy to give me a pass to get into the show. She has one for her daughter, so I'll be her daughter for the day. Of course, the badge won't have my company name on it, it will have hers, but at least it will get me in the door.

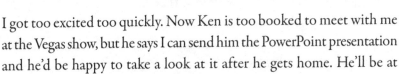

I got too excited too quickly. Now Ken is too booked to meet with me at the Vegas show, but he says I can send him the PowerPoint presentation and he'd be happy to take a look at it after he gets home. He'll be at the trade show, I'll be at the trade show, and there won't be even five minutes for us to meet?

FOR GOD AND COUNTRY

October 19, 2010. The Crystal Cathedral Ministries—the California megachurch, with its TV show and towering glass basilica—filed for bankruptcy. Meanwhile, GM workers were left wondering how their pay got slashed from $58,000 a year to $30,000 at a Michigan auto plant that received $770 million in tax incentives funded by a $50 billion government bailout.

I buy my $317 round trip ticket to Vegas. Talk about a gamble! I'll travel in the morning and return that same night, but I have to do it. I ask Ken's assistant if she can give me a number to reach him, but she won't have one until he gets a calling card for his cell. I give her my number and ask for any clues about how to find him. She says he loves coffee, so I should try the Starbucks, and that he'll be traveling with his wife and her twin sister. Now I've got what I need to stalk the guy in the booths of the companies he works with. Nice.

The pregnant woman in Australia tells me that her blankyclips arrived safely and she loves them. I'm hoping this is a good omen before I leave for Vegas and try to hunt Ken down.

The easy part is getting on an airplane and flying to Vegas and taking a cab to the convention center. The hard part is approaching the check-in desk and handing over my badge with my friend's daughter's name. If they question me, I'll be completely busted, and I'm queasy as I hand the badge to the woman behind the desk. She checks me in, puts the lanyard on the badge, and wishes me a good show. Suddenly I'm entering the very same hall where I exhibited two years ago, the biggest baby trade show there is.

The place looks very familiar, and I'm surprised that it feels so disappointing not to be an exhibitor. But I got in, and that's what counts. First stop, find my friend who gave me the badge and thank her for her help. It's surreal to walk around the show and see companies I saw two years ago and realize how much I've learned in these past two years.

The day becomes quite social as I visit with folks I met back in 2008. I have to explain to everyone that I'm not an exhibitor but came to talk to some distributors. And then begins the hunt. I go to the booths of various companies that Keen works with, hoping to track down Brian, and also to the booth of the Australian distributor Bambini International, hoping to track down Ken. The day flies by, and I'm shocked when in the afternoon I'm actually sitting on a couch with Brian talking about blankyclip. This is when he lets me know that the retail price that would work for my two-clip package in a Target would be $12. Now I'm really shocked.

So, the big box retail stores in the U.S. are not in the realm of possible at all, if this is what a distributor who deals with those stores is telling me. I can't sell them my product for practically what it costs me to make it.

Ken eludes me, even with the twins clue. I have mixed feelings at this point and am exhausted from running around showing random buyers my samples out of my carry-on bag like I've smuggled in some contraband. Which technically I have. I have some new contacts at a few boutiques to follow up with, and it was fun to visit with some of the people who were first-time exhibitors in the New Products row with me two years ago. My friend with the lunch bags and backpacks is still doing well but feeling stressed about how she'll keep going. I visit the New Products row where there's no product that resembles mine, and I feel for those folks who have come with huge expectations like I did. The day ends at the airport as I wait for my flight home eating chocolate.

The new, new factory tells me they received the clips I sent, and they understand my comments on the last samples. New ones coming soon, they promise. I have to keep all that going in case of a miracle.

I'm back in touch with Ken's wonderfully supportive assistant. I let her know that my Australian customer loves her blankyclips and gave some to friends as gifts and wouldn't it be nice if more Australian women could get their hands on my product? She tells me that Ken is in New Zealand and gives me the name of a distributor there that she recommends I reach out to. She says Ken has a lot of following up to do since the trade show, but thanks for staying in touch.

My Mexican contact wants her distribution agreement, as she's meeting some retailers next week, so I finally get that off to her. The agreement basically says that she is the exclusive distributor for blankyclip in Mexico.

I follow up with some stores I've sold to in the past, hoping to prompt reorders. I learn that Baby Love, the Florida store that had been around for forty years, closed its doors for good this month. I guess their failure to reorder wasn't personal.

GONE, BABY, GONE

The blankyclip Company's very first customer, the Bay Area's Lullaby Lane, which had been in operation since the 1970s, went out of business. USA Baby, a retail chain with seventy stores, closed forty-five of them. Bellini Baby, once a national chain, shed all its stores (and employees) except those on the East Coast. Bellini Baby in Irvine, California, erstwhile customer of The blankyclip Company, ceased to exist.

November 2010. I receive an email from my potential Canadian distributor. He loves the product, loves the website. And he needs my price to him to be $5.50 for the two-clip pack that will retail for $19.95. He explains the breakdown of his costs, which include duty fees, broker fees, freight charges, and currency charges. He needs room for a twenty-nine percent markup so he can get to his wholesale price of $9.95. Can I make this price point? Sure, if I were paying the factory about $0.50 a clip! I still have the cost of the packaging and my freight costs and my warehousing and all the rest. Now it looks like I can't go the route of using a distributor when there are so many other costs involved.

Angela emails me to say that she can't do anything about the chargeback from Bed Bath & Beyond as it's standard policy not to pay an invoice for goods received if the inventory they have is not selling. They take no responsibility. Caveat vendor.

Time for some distraction, so we're going to the movies! *Tangled* is playing nearby, and the kids are game, but the scary witch and her evil scissors are more than they can take, and they both beg to leave. I'm not sure if it's the exorbitant price of their tickets or the fact that Gary and I need this respite to last as long as it can, but we don't leave. We want them to make it to the happy ending. If we leave before then, aren't we teaching them to run away from their fear and that they're not strong enough for challenging moments? It is a mighty celebration, indeed, when we sit down to some Chinese food for a late lunch. They are feeling victorious, or so we project, and we all laugh as we retell the funny moments between Rapunzel and Flynn.

After the respite, I have a new thought. I'll get some header cards printed up and see if I can sell the two-clip packs on my website or in stores. George, my sweet hang tag and ribbon maker, says he can do them for about $5 apiece. Yikes. Eventually I find a printer in the Valley that can do them for a little over $1 apiece. The only adjustment we would need to make is to keep the corners square instead of rounded. I can live with that for sure, but when the sample card stock arrives, it's way too thin for my purposes and will not hold two clips. A total bust.

It's been a while since I thought about Toys "R" Us, so I send them an email to ask about submitting my vendor presentation to them. Within a few days I get a reply saying that they do not accept offers to look at new products because they have their own in-house designers and a large vendor base.

Bob the distributor calls me from Canada to say that he's changed his mind and is no longer interested in purchasing blankyclips. From what I gather, he gave them to some older kids (his grandchildren?), and they discovered that the tension was too loose to keep their superhero capes around their necks. Damn, because holding capes in place is exactly why I invented this product.

Amazon orders another twelve sets of blankyclips. Whoop-dee-doo. I'm in an ungrateful state of mind.

TURKEY DAY

Over the past thirty days, Crabtree & Evelyn, MGM Studios, and Simmons Bedding filed for bankruptcy protection. Unemployment, which had hovered at 9.5% since July, spiked to 9.8%—and this after we'd been out of the Great Recession for almost a year and a half. Any sign of recovery faded just as we entered the holiday season.

Another pass from another Canadian distributor because they like to represent lines with a bigger range of products to make it more worthwhile for the time they spend. Being a one-product company bites me in the ass yet again.

I hear back from Ken's nice Australian assistant who says they've finalized their line at the moment but will consider new products again in about six months. Also, she has a few questions, which start out simply in terms of price and minimum order but get more unanswerable when she wants to know what sales have been like in the stores I currently supply. She tells me that if a product doesn't turn over more than $20,000 a year in sales, it is closely reviewed. Also— here we go again—they are careful about taking on single products rather than a range of products from one supplier. The real kicker is hearing that she noticed my product on Amazon, and they don't like to consider brands that sell on sites like that because they believe it's not beneficial to the brand.

OH NO THEY DIDN'T

November 17, 2010. A bankruptcy judge ordered Bank of America to pay back $500 million it somehow acquired from the accounts of Lehman Brothers a few weeks before Lehman went under in 2008. Asked about the $500 million hit, Bank of America responded by saying, "Don't you worry about me. I've got a plan to claw some of that money back."

So, I'm out of international distributor options. I'm a single-product supplier. My Southeast sales reps dropped me. My cardboard backing is too floppy. But at least it's the holidays.

December 13, 2010. At first, I think I must be reading the letter incorrectly, but after rereading it and rereading it, it's painfully clear that Bank of America is demanding that I pay back my entire line of credit (at this point we're talking $102,000) by Christmas of next year. This can't be possible. There was never a "date due" on my line of credit, and I've been making my monthly payments on time, and how in the world can they expect me to pay this back in a year?

I make an appointment to see my accountant.

11

Chapter Eleven. Really?

*J*ust *Tell Them You're From Scarsdale* is a one-woman show I wrote and performed at the Solo Arts Theatre in New York and the Hudson Theatre in Los Angeles, long before kids and blankyclips and patents and ominous letters from Bank of America. Here is one of my favorite characters from the play:

> A *PSYCHIC* stares mystically into coffee grounds. Then snaps her head up and proclaims:
>
> Okay. . . Here's here two things good is coming for you. See? One, two. Okay. How many brothers and sisters you have? Two? Aha. Four. Whaz the two? Two married maybe? Nobody married? Whaz the two? Are you born in February? Also here you have one, two. Nobody born in February? Was your mother—she married twice? I don't know what the two for you. Okay. Now you have—you're lucky. Okay. You going to move. In job, I think. You going to go someplace. For actress. You going away. C. What's C?

California maybe? No, I don't think so. What's C for you? Cinema? Cinema maybe. Okay and good for you. You going to move some . . . some thing. Okay. And good luck for you. Okay. Now. You are going to have two kids, but you scared to have kids. Why? DO IT! Okay, you work is going to be very good. It takes time and good for you. Yah . . . good luck for you. You have the fish. Good luck. Something difficult is coming for you but you get it. You going to fight for something and you get it. You know what to fight? To work for dat? And you get it. Okay. Who's A? Ah, your name? You going to help yourself. You going to push yourself because you want to do and you want to get it. Good luck. You have surgery to do? Going to small surgery for fingers or legs. OK? Which . . . acting actress in what? Which movie? Yeah, yeah. Because I see cinema. I think you able to get it. Go for slow and good luck. And you have big fish. Big fish. See the fish? Now the bird is back here because the fish is not yet. But you work it. Good luck to you. Put on you all the time garlic and salt nothing is happening. Don't worry. Be up. Because after you going to pick the big fish. This is the ting. You have the fish, but you have the black bird. Why the black bird? Because you don't have money. When you have your money you go for the Y, victory. You are Sagittarius? No. Taurus. It's good. Taurus is strong. Good. Be strong. Don't . . . cut. Go. Continue. Okay? Good luck. You're welcome. Okay.

When I visited that psychic in Queens, New York, so many years ago, I wanted some reassurance that my acting career was going to blossom. Well, she did figure out that cinema begins with the letter C. And looking back at that coffee-grounds reading, she also managed to predict the existence of my two children and that I would push myself, and have a fish (all that sushi?), and she only missed my birthday by seven Zodiac signs . . . But now I need more tangible guidance.

It's amazing how casual my accountant is when he tells me that yes, indeed, my business is over. There's no way I can pay this loan back in a year, so it's very simple: time to file for bankruptcy. He explains, "Many of my clients are receiving similar letters, and really, in a nutshell, this signals the end of small business in America." One of his clients has a $500,000 loan, and he's in big trouble. I feel slightly better that mine is a mere $102,000. But not that much better. Bankruptcy? That wasn't the plan at all. He tells me to go see a lawyer because it's time to say goodbye to blankyclip. I am devastated.

A boutique in Hawaii reaches out to tell me that they really like blankyclip but won't be buying any new products until the new year. They'll consider it then. Great.

And how about more ridiculous news? The new, new factory emails me to say that they can't produce more samples and they aren't the right factory for blankyclip. They inform me that their raw materials cost has gone up twenty percent and their labor costs thirty percent. As mandated by Chinese law, the minimum wage was increased. I can't begrudge the workers a pay raise from $180 to $230 *per month*, but that doesn't cushion the impact on the other side of the world. The new, new factory's biggest issue is that they can't guarantee they can produce the product with the quality I'm looking for. They put it like this: "Your item is for baby line, actually need very strictly for mass production, But most our factories will treat it as norm toys, so I am afraid that they could Not produced as confirmed samples. They willing to produce toys with big quantities But simply model." So, after all the back and forth and bad samples, it's over with these guys. I'm at square one with having a factory that can make blankyclips if I should need more, which I evidently won't.

I begin a search for a bankruptcy attorney and get some referrals. All this work, all these years, for nothing? I was about to sell blankyclips in Mexico, for goodness' sake. And even though things are really tough right now, it was supposed to get better. I wonder if the person at Bank of America who decided to change the terms of my letter of credit has any inkling of what this has done to me and my dreams and all of my years trying to create this business.

It's the holidays, but I'm not feeling very cheery. It's hard to feel cheery when you're trudging to the office of a bankruptcy attorney, no matter how highly recommended. I'm a little surprised that his office is so run down. It doesn't feel good here at all, but I'm here for a bad reason, so I guess that's to be expected. I show him the letter from Bank of America, and he asks to see my loan documents. After studying them briefly, he says, "You won't be able to file for corporate bankruptcy because you signed the loan papers as the guarantor, which was a necessity for getting the loan. So, what this is about is personal bankruptcy."

Excuse me?

I incorporated The blankyclip Company to protect myself, so what's he talking about? He tells me that because I was applying for a small business loan and it was a new business, the bank required that I *personally* sign for the money and be *personally* responsible for paying it back. Suddenly I feel nauseous. I barely make it to the bathroom before I start bawling. This is terrifying news. How did I not know that I was personally responsible for this money? I formed a corporation and did all the right things, and it doesn't friggin' matter? It feels like my life is over. I can't talk to this sweaty, badly dressed, highly recommended bankruptcy attorney any longer, so I leave.

I spend the night processing what this horrible lawyer told me and decide to meet with another attorney. This time I'm in a high-rise building, and the office is much nicer. I'm able to have an actual conversation with this attorney, and we get into what exactly it means to file personal bankruptcy. He says, "Because you're married, this will affect your husband as well. The laws changed in 2005, and now creditors can go after your spouse's assets." He recommends that we immediately spend whatever savings we have on things like rent for the coming year or Dagny's preschool. "It's really no big deal to file for bankruptcy," he says in an attempt to comfort me. "Someone in Los Angeles does it every seven minutes, practically." He's joking and making light of my plight, and I'm once again fighting back the tears. This is a big deal. I don't want to lose what little we have. I don't want our credit ruined. I've learned more from this attorney than from the first one, but I don't think he's the right guy for me either. I'll keep looking.

A friend suggests I write about this whole experience. She believes there's a book in it. "I think it's a great idea to write about it," she says, "both as a catharsis for you and as a cultural artifact of these times and the economy."

January 2011. I reach out to a third lawyer, but he has a consultation fee of $350 which seems pretty cost-prohibitive for me. Doesn't he know why I want to see him?

A few small orders come in from a couple of boutiques and Amazon. Mommy blogs continue to ask for samples to review. This commercial activity feels strange since I still don't know how I'm handling Bank of America and there's no factory in sight for doing a reorder now that prices have gone up in China. I'm in a weird limbo but carrying on. It's bittersweet to get a $208 order from a new boutique that's excited to carry blankyclips.

The $350 lawyer calls to follow up. I'm tempted to explain to him the paradox of charging $350 to someone who's coming to you to figure out what to do because of a demand to pay back an enormous amount of money she doesn't have, but I confine myself to saying I've already been advised that I'll need to file for personal bankruptcy because I was the guarantor on the loan, and then I hear magical words over the phone.

"You know," he says, "there's another option."

There is?

"You can negotiate a settlement."

What? Why is this the first time I've heard about such an option? I make an appointment to meet face to face.

This attorney's office is in a lovely building in Beverly Hills, and he makes me laugh, and I feel like I am not the same person who sat with the horribly dressed first attorney. Here I learn about a strategy to avoid bankruptcy, and that banks will settle because they prefer to get something rather than nothing. He makes me feel hopeful. He lays out a plan. I'll not make my full loan payments to BofA each month (as I've been doing all along), and I'll keep paying less and less as the year progresses. By the end of the year, they'll be willing to settle with me. The important steps now are to paint the picture of a company (woman) that in no possible way can pay back $102,000, but this company (woman) is willing to pay something and is trying her best. The dismantling of it all now begins. A settlement won't happen until just before the loan is due because that's how these things go. This attorney is confident and genuine and treats me with respect—and more importantly, he gets why a personal bankruptcy involving me and my husband isn't the way to go.

To cut back on my business expenses, we're going to clear out the storage unit and put all remaining boxes and trade show items in our garage at home. This is a bit daunting, and I'm grateful to have a willing and helpful husband. Before we can do that, we need to clean out the garage, which means figuring out what to throw away or give away or sell and putting in more shelving. Then we shuttle the boxes over from the unit. I'm finding it hard not to be sad about this kind of consolidating. It represents shutting down and facing the fact that the business won't be growing. I'll have that reminder every time I go into the garage. I try to console myself by remembering that I'm not the only one going through this.

So that's it. I'll keep my inventory at home. I can't make any more blankyclips, so I'll sell what I have. And I'll follow my attorney's advice to accept and manage the slow death of my dream.

A nice big order comes in from the website. A sheep gift set, a duck gift set, and all three sets of clips. It's from a repeat customer who just welcomed another grandchild. She's so excited to get the order to her daughter that she contacts me about overnighting it. Always ambivalence with every step.

March 1, 2011. For what feels like a very, very long time—nearly as long as the seven years it's been since I came up with the idea for a cute clip that might keep my baby's blanket from falling off his stroller—I stare at the cursor blinking against the empty Word document background. My fingertips tickle the keyboard. I pull them away and then try again, and I start typing: "Having a baby at my age—or any age—ends your life as you know it."

The rest of 2011. One fine day my third patent is approved. Very funny, universe!

I feel like I'm walking around with a big secret, pretending to be a woman with her own you-go-girl business when really I'm a woman with a master plan to destroy it. I'm still hoping that this letter from Bank of America was a mistake and they'll call me any day now to apologize for the misunderstanding.

Here's what happens when you start to send in payments on a bank loan but you don't pay in full. An unpleasant person phones you and says in a threatening tone that the bank will call the loan "due in full" if you are not up to date on your payments. After one such call, I talk to the new buyer at Right Start, and she tells me they're interested in the duck blankyclips for their nine stores and their website. Are these two things really happening at the same time?

Mainly these days I am writing the book you're now reading.

More hilarity ensues as Amazon places two orders. Nothing huge, but an indication that my product is selling on their site.

You would think I was BofA's only customer. They call me again to tell me I better pay them what I owe them. I've gone from making three quarters of my payment to half. I would call the tone of today's communication aggressive. My lawyer says I should not worry and should keep explaining that I'm doing everything I can, but my business is just not doing well.

As uncomfortable as these calls are, they're nothing compared to the knock on my front door followed by the words "I'm here from Bank of America." I look through the peephole and see a man with a mustache (never a good sign) holding an envelope. My imagination tells me that this man is here to take me to jail, and I may never see my kids again. I open the door, and he hands me the envelope and walks away.

My heart is racing as I read a threatening letter from the bank that basically says I better pay them what I owe them. I should stop sending payments that are less than what my monthly statement shows due.

I call my lawyer and tell him what has just happened. Is this legal?

Who was that guy in the mustache? The lawyer tells me calmly, "What you just experienced is called a dunning letter. It's meant to intimidate you so you pay them. This kind of stuff is standard." Really? At my home? My business has a different address. That's pretty creepy, but he tells me not to worry about it at all.

Another call two days later from BofA. They are letting me know that a certified letter is on its way to me. They suggest I get a loan from somewhere else in order to pay them off. Wow. This sounds like such a ridiculous request that I can't believe they even thought to try it. I send them another incomplete payment.

Meanwhile, my days are filled with a high percentage of mommy time. One morning, I drop Eli off at school and head to the Madrona Marsh where Dagny is learning all about seeds. They're showing her the ones that end up creating plants, but I'm thinking that there are many other kinds as well. There are ideas that lead to inventions. And there are moments with our kids at a marsh. She enjoys her lunch of mini raviolis, and I take in how thankful I am for the miraculous way she was created.

On our fifteenth anniversary we take the kids out for a Vietnamese dinner. The kids are healthy. Gary is employed, although underemployed is more accurate. My company is being forced to wind down because of a letter I got in the mail. But we are somehow feeling at peace tonight.

I check my banking info online, and my mouth drops open. In the spot where it says how much I owe them for my line of credit, it says 0. It should say $102,000. So, here's what I come up with. Recently Bank of America announced it would be letting another 3,500 employees go (this after eliminating 2,500 jobs earlier this year.) I am convinced that one of them has decided to stick it to BofA, and in a final act of defiance has erased my debt. I could not be more grateful.

Then another letter from Bank of America arrives (we are such pen pals), and this one says that my loan was sold to another company. I guess my disgruntled employee theory was a stretch. But this means that we will not be negotiating with BofA, so it sounds bad. I call my lawyer, and again he tells me not to worry. Easy for *him* to say.

I must say that I'm finding it really enjoyable to write about the early stages of my business when there was so much promise. Before foreclosures and jobs disappearing, there was just working hard to make a dream a reality. I also distract myself from the woes of my dissolving business by volunteering at my son's public school. We are planning fundraising events to help the school out with money it badly needs.

Everything is a negotiation. My lawyer has agreed to handle my case for $3,750. I know it could be much worse, but it still feels like a lot of money. Money I have to pay for a deal where I don't have to pay the full amount of my loan that was originally not required to be repaid in one lump sum except that my bank decided it needed some cash pronto.

Am I really organizing a carnival fundraiser at my son's school? On top of moving into a rental house that has more space? (Without neighbors living above us! Yay!) Both of these events are filling my days and turning my focus away from selling blankyclips. Yes, I'll ship the dozen bears for the Amazon order that just came in, but I do have to get back to packing up our home. Then there's painting the walls of my kids' new bedrooms (their own rooms!) in the colors they each picked out at Home Depot. We leave the muted beige used for sharing a room and enter the world of pink and blue.

I join Dagny's preschool class on a trip to a nursing home. The kids are there to sing Chanukah songs, which they do adorably. I watch as the elderly light up from hearing kids' voices. I don't know what my five-year-old girl is processing about singing in a nursing home, and I don't know what the residents are thinking about during this holiday time, but for me it is a profound moment. Time marches on whether we build a successful business selling blankyclips or we do not. Just be present and grateful, Adrienne.

We are nearing the end of the line of credit drama. My lawyer asks me to fill out a draft bankruptcy petition. He explains that I am filling it out not because I will file for bankruptcy but to show my new creditors that I have nothing. No assets. No money or real estate or stocks. Fortunately, I am not required to assign value to my greatest assets. Their names are Gary, Eli, and Dagny. These are my riches. Thankfully, these will not be taken away from me. Thankfully, this family has made me truly abundant. If having two healthy children and a husband who adores me is the best I will ever do, I am a lucky woman.

The creditor company sends my lawyer a final offer. They suggest that instead of filing for bankruptcy and ruining my credit (thanks for your thoughtfulness) I should pay out a lump sum of $15,000. My lawyer thinks this is a great deal. So, I have successfully driven my company into the ground in order to show that I am unable to pay off the loan in full. It doesn't feel like a great deal, but I'll take it. Wish I could find the guy (assuming it's a guy) at Bank of America who came up with the strategy of requiring the mandatory full payback of lines of credit within the year which forced so many of us small businesses to shut down. Who knows how many marriages did not survive those letters that were sent to thousands of people with lines of credit at Bank of America? Who knows how many kids saw their parents go through hell and maybe got the brunt of their frustrations? We are all connected.

An action leads to a reaction.

My baby's blanket fell onto the street and got dirty, so I invented a blankyclip.

Epilogue

I finished my book! Draft after draft, it has been a work in progress, and now it's time for me to let it go.

My kids are fourteen and seventeen, developing their prefrontal cortexes and challenging Gary and me at every turn. (We like to say it's one thing to admire a Dagny Taggart and another thing to raise one.) Dagny is incredibly driven, hard-working, and athletic, with soccer being her biggest passion. Eli is an avid reader and navigates smoothly between being a science-obsessed kid to performing in his school's musicals. They both blow me away with their writing abilities. Gary and I are going on twenty-eight years together. If there is a lottery in life for partners, I won it big time. He's completely devoted to our kids and me, and while he may not build dollhouses, he makes our concerns his concerns. We usually find a reason to laugh with the kids at the dinner table when he comes home from running the operations of a home goods company.

After I settled on a figure to pay off my business loan, blankyclip came to a screeching halt. The best I could do was sell the occasional order from my website while I focused instead on raising my children and writing this book. There are few blankyclips left in the garage at this point, many more blankets, and I have been maintaining my patents just in case.

I am happy I have been there for all of the activities in my kids' lives. I created talent shows and made many library runs and watched lots of soccer games. The years go by quickly, and at some point soon the kids will be out of the house. I have made their development and running our family my chief business. While it still can feel "not enough" at times, in my heart I have done my best. And in the end, that's all we can ever do.

Bank of America is doing fine, too, in case anyone is wondering. At last check, they were ranked the second largest banking institution in the U.S. and the ninth largest financial service company in the world.

Acknowledgments

Recently, my daughter was surprised to learn that I love reading the acknowledgments in books. It feels like a peek inside the author's heart. Here's who I want to thank, so you can take a peek inside mine:

Mostly, Gary. I am so lucky to be sharing all the highs and lows with a man I deeply love and admire so very much. Thank you, Gary, for working so hard and keeping our family your top priority always. You believed in me wholeheartedly as an entrepreneur and equally as an author. Your input into this book is immeasurable, and I know this book exists because of you.

I want to also thank my children, Eli and Dagny. You have given me the opportunity to experience such profound love. The lift-a-car-by-one-hand kind. Thank you for all the ways you have made me proud. And for being the best blankyclip video actors. I adore you both.

While I may live many miles away (for now) from the other members of my family, I think about you daily and am grateful for your love always.

Thank you to all of my "blankyclip angels." Thank you to everyone who invested in my dream, either with money or time. Thank you for your emotional and practical support. I could never have built my business without all of your generosity. Thank you from the bottom of my heart to: Carrie P., Jeff B., Ed S., Shawni M., Jeff A., John W., Stephanie G., Marc G., Lee D., John S., Jen K., Sonny C., Jon N.,

Beth S., Bess R., Renae P., Mark T., Rob M., Margot B., and Lori D.

I want to thank my friends for reading early drafts and giving me such good feedback on how to make this book better: Jennifer Copaken, Tami Harris, Sarah Cooper, Jessica Prince and Tracy Paladini. A very big thank you to Laura Carson for telling me I should write this in the first place. Thank you to my friends who became my Los Angeles family and encouraged me to keep writing, Stacee Longo and Emy Budris. Thank you to Joy Johannessen, my first editor, for removing so many ALL CAPS and for your incredible contribution to this book.

Thank you, finally, to everyone at Acorn Publishing, for all of your support in bringing this book into the world. I am grateful to have had you by my side during the entire publishing process.

Made in the USA
Monee, IL
19 November 2021

82510975R00142